STORMS *and* DESERTS

How God Reveals Himself to Us in the Midst of Our Crisis

Elizabeth Viera Talbot

Pacific Press® Publishing Association
Nampa, Idaho | www.pacificpress.com

Cover design: Christian Media Outlet
Cover design resources: Adobe Stock
Interior design: Aaron Troia

Copyright © 2025 by Pacific Press® Publishing Association
Printed in the United States of America
All rights reserved

Edited by Aivars Ozolins, PhD, and Timothy Pilli

The author assumes full responsibility for the accuracy of all facts and quotations as cited in this book.

Unless otherwise indicated, all Scripture quotations are from the New American Standard Bible®, Copyright © 1960, 1971, 1977, 1995, by The Lockman Foundation. Used by permission. All rights reserved.

Scripture quotations marked *The Message* are from *The Message*, copyright © 1993, 2002, 2018 by Eugene H. Peterson. Used by permission of NavPress. All rights reserved. Represented by Tyndale House Publishers.

Scripture quotations marked NASB are from the New American Standard Bible®, Copyright © 1960, 1971, 1977, 1995, 2020 by The Lockman Foundation. Used by permission. All rights reserved.

Scripture quotations marked NET are from the New English Translation (NET Bible®), copyright ©1996–2017 by Biblical Studies Press, LLC. All rights reserved. Used by permission.

Scripture quotations marked NIV are taken from THE HOLY BIBLE, NEW INTERNATIONAL VERSION® NIV® Copyright © 1973, 1978, 1984, 2011 by Biblica, Inc.® Used by permission. All rights reserved worldwide.

Scripture quotations marked NKJV are taken from the New King James Version®. Copyright © 1982 by Thomas Nelson. Used by permission. All rights reserved.

To order additional copies of this book, call toll-free 1-800-765-6955,
or visit AdventistBookCenter.com.

Library of Congress Cataloging-in-Publication Data

Names: Talbot, Elizabeth Viera author
Title: Storms and deserts : how God reveals himself to us in the midst of our crisis / Elizabeth Viera Talbot.
Description: Nampa, Idaho : Pacific Press Publishing Association, [2025]
Identifiers: LCCN 2025017067 (print) | LCCN 2025017068 (ebook) | ISBN 9780816370931 trade paperback | ISBN 9780816370948 ebook
Subjects: LCSH: Providence and government of God—Biblical teaching | Suffering—Biblical teaching | Trust in God—Biblical teaching | Christian life—Biblical teaching | Christian life—Seventh-Day Adventist authors
Classification: LCC BS544 .T35 2025 (print) | LCC BS544 (ebook) | DDC 231—dc23/eng/20250606
LC record available at https://lccn.loc.gov/2025017067
LC ebook record available at https://lccn.loc.gov/2025017068

July 2025

DEDICATION

I dedicate this book to all the people who have helped me take care of my husband during his prolonged neurological decline caused by a brutal terminal illness:

Jorge T., Joaquin, Pablo, Pacho, Timothy, Sergio, Wicleff, Nestor, and Jorge Andino. You have all been answers to my prayers. The process has been difficult, yet you've stayed with it. I am convinced that God has sent you to me in one of the most trying crises of my life. Thank you for your willingness to be used by God. And a deep heart-felt thank you to my closest friends who have journeyed with me: Aivars, Hazel, and Petar. I don't know how I would have made it this far without you.

I also dedicate this book to my husband Patrick, a passionate preacher of God's grace who can no longer speak. I am so thankful that we are saved by the actions of the One who lived a perfect life in our place and gave up that life on the cross for our sins—our risen and soon-coming Savior. Dear Patrick: I can't wait to see you restored to full health in the heavenly Promised Land.

I also dedicate this book to the close-knit Jesus 101 team that has supported me during these times of struggle: Casey, Giani, Chris, Gabriel, Joel, and Manuel.

And to Jesus, my Redeemer, who just won't let me go, no matter how imperfectly human my life has been. My dear Jesus: your grace is more than sufficient. The last few years have taught me so much more about your love and compassion as I wrestled with huge questions and pain. I now know that you will never leave me nor abandon me. I am eternally thankful.

Other books by Elizabeth Viera Talbot
After God's Heart
I Will Give You Rest
Jesus Wins!
Surprised by Love
The Battle Belongs to the Lord
The Exodus Journey

Books in Spanish
Confinanza para el viaje de la vida
Conforme al Corazón de Dios
Sorprendidos por amor
Yo os hare descansar

Contents

Introduction	6
1. The UNIMAGINABLE Storm	9
2. The UNTHINKABLE Journey	18
3. The UNLIKELY Place	27
4. The UNFAIR Pits	35
5. The UNYIELDING Giants	46
6. The UNBEARABLE Grief	56
7. The UNDENIABLE Crisis	65
8. The UNEXPECTED Wilderness	77
9. The UNNERVING Detour	86
10. The UNSETTLING Wind	95
11. The UNAVOIDABLE Shipwreck	104
12. The UNCHARTED Desert	114
Conclusion	126

INTRODUCTION

Our stories contain plenty of pain and suffering. Some unexpected and some that we saw coming a mile away. I'd like to be able to tell you that with God you will live a life without crisis, but I can't, because we live in a world of sin and suffering. Deep pain is part of our lot on this side of eternity. Our temptation is to share only the good, the picture-perfect part of our lives. At least that is what we regularly see in each other's social media, then we wonder how come everyone else's life seems to be working out so much better than ours. Yet, just as the moon has a dark side that is not visible from earth, there is a side in us too that we typically don't want to share: our "human" side, our struggles, our confusion, our doubts, our desperation, our wrestling with God. Yet sharing this darker side of ours is exactly what offers others encouragement and hope as we all face the challenges of this broken world.

I must confess that the books highlighting never ending spiritual victories do little for me, because that is not real life. At least not my life. That's why the Bible offers us such a powerful encouragement and motivation. God's inspired book speaks to our real lives. It is filled with stories of human beings who, just like us, struggled with confusion, made unnecessary detours, fell into dark pits and found themselves entangled in sins. Yet God walked with them in their humanity through their crises, and His love for them never wavered. God understands us more than we do ourselves. He understands our circumstances, our unique pains, our tears.

INTRODUCTION

In this book I want to reflect on some of the crises experienced by Bible characters, along with some of my own, as day by day I continue to learn about God's grace in ways that I never imagined possible. You might be surprised by some of the things I share in this book. But I believe that in reading these pages you will discover a good companion, a kindred spirit that will offer encouragement and hope as we all deal with similar struggles and our own brokenness.

I wrote this book from a gut level, a place of vulnerability that I pray will bless you. I have resonated deeply with Palmer's perspective in this matter: "When you share your story of struggle, you offer me companionship in mine, and that's the most powerful soul medicine I know. Here, it seems to me, is yet another parallel between faith and writing. The God I'm familiar with does not work like a GPS, but accompanies me as I try to grope my way through the darkest of dark places. I think a good writer can do at least a little bit of that for the reader; writing from a deeply human place of vulnerability is an act of compassion, as well as self-therapy."* I must admit that I don't consider myself a good writer, but I did write this book from a deeply human place of vulnerability. I trust that you will read it, and re-read it, and highlight it, underline it and share it. In addition, Jesus 101 is planning to release a video series in 2026, that will accompany this book chapter by chapter (see QR code below).

Storms and Deserts is a book that revisits biblical stories of actual fierce tempests and scorching wildernesses that developed into stories of emotional and spiritual turmoil for those who went through them. And yet in the midst of those crises, God revealed Himself to His children in unprecedented ways.

The same has happened, and continues to happen, in my life. And I am more and more convinced that God can be fully trusted, that He is not overwhelmed by the deep and awkward questions of our hearts, nor is He dazed by our mishaps. And even though we will not find answers to all of our questions while on this earth, I am convinced, more than ever, of this truth: "Where sin increased, grace increased all the more" (Romans 5:20). Where we took detours, His love increased all the more. Where darkness fell, His light increased all the more. Where confusion increased, His compassion increased all the more. Of this I am absolutely sure.

I pray that this book may become a real companion for you as you discover more and more of God's ever-increasing grace in the journey of life. And remember that God, by His grace and His redeeming purposes, is able to turn absolutely everything, even our worst moments, into a blessing for us and others (see Romans 8:28). Isn't that amazing? So, my dear fellow pilgrim, let's start our voyage together: you, me and our compassionate and graceful God. Get ready for quite a journey. Here we go!

---

* Parker Palmer, *On the Brink of Everything: Grace, Gravity, and Getting Old* (Oakland, CA: Berrett-Koehler, 2018), 97.

1. THE UNIMAGINABLE STORM

Unimaginable: Difficult or impossible to believe; inconceivable.
—dictionary.com

There are storms, and then there are *storms*. Some are quite ordinary, something to be expected more or less routinely. But there are others that go beyond our imagination, that sneak up on us and catch us totally unprepared because we didn't even know this type of storm existed. My husband and I were about to experience one of those.

We were headed to a prestigious research center. For a long time we had been looking for answers to our questions about his illness. Anything that could outline the road ahead would be helpful. We had been feeling our way in the dark. All we had was a vague idea about the area of the brain that was affected. The illness caused him to lose most of his speech, to lose the ability to walk without falling, and to be unable to swallow liquids without coughing.

After a few tests the doctor said, "We know exactly what it is. It's a very, very rare neurological condition called progressive supranuclear palsy or PSP."

He had to repeat the whole thing several times before it registered in my brain: Progressive supranuclear palsy. *Progressive? Supranuclear? What?* I had never heard of such a thing . . . and that's how our unimaginable storm was given a name.

Having told us that it was, in fact, a progressive, incurable, and therefore terminal disease, the research center could only email us a PSP brochure that gave us an idea of the symptoms, the prognosis, and the progressive areas of decline, among other things. At that point the brochure read like a precise story of our lives. A truly unimaginable storm, never experienced before! I didn't even know storms like that existed. And yet this storm was real, and we are still in it.

What is the name of your storm? Or are you still looking for a name? Perhaps all you know is that whatever you are going through is inconceivable, unimaginable, and that you never saw it coming. Noah's unimaginable storm also involved something he had never heard of before: water from above and water from below that would cover everything. Nobody had seen or heard of such a thing. This inconceivable storm was given a name: the Flood. Noah had no control over it and no say in the matter except to believe God and accept His way through it. Just like us.

No control, whatsoever?
The story of this unimaginable storm is told in Genesis 6:11–9:17. By now Noah is 600 years old. That's the age when you think you are finally getting a grip on life. Yet a totally unexpected message comes from God to Noah. God saw that the earth and all flesh were corrupt (Genesis 6:12). This statement stands in contrast to Genesis 1:31, where God saw His creation, and it was *very good*. Now corruption and violence had filled the earth He had created. God told Noah that a flood was coming to do away with the wickedness of humanity, and Noah was to build a strange vessel: "Make for yourself an *ark* . . . with compartments" (Genesis 6:14, NASB; emphasis added).

THE UNIMAGINABLE STORM

Noah had never heard of a flood. But I bet he was overjoyed to hear that God had a plan to get him and his family through this unthinkable crisis.

Noah was instructed to build something that we may call a gigantic boat, but I am not even sure it qualifies as a boat. Here's why. God gave Noah very specific and detailed instructions about how to build the boat; in other words He gave him a blueprint. The issue is not in the details of the blueprint but in what's missing: there was no propulsion system nor a rudder. There was no means to power the boat or to steer it.

Wait, what? No power or steering? How was Noah going to control where this thing was going? He was not. And that was the plan. He and his family would have to be fully surrendered to God's control. Only God would be able to direct their path. The people going through the storm had no control whatsoever. And that's the way it always is with unimaginable storms. We can't control them . . . but *God* has a way already prepared for His children.

But God . . .

I am so thankful for God's *buts*. He turns bad news into good news with a *but*. He has done it for me so many times. And this time He did it for Noah: "*But* I will establish *My covenant* with you; and you shall enter the *ark*—you and your sons and your wife, and your sons' wives with you." (verse 18; emphasis added).

This is the first time the word *covenant* is used in the Bible, even though God had already made a unilateral pact of redemption with humanity in Eden (see Genesis 3:15). Noah then learns that all corrupt flesh was going to be destroyed, *but*

God had made a way out for him and his family. The Hebrew word for the ark, which was God's method of survival in this storm, is the same word used for the little basket in which the mother of Moses placed her baby to float in the river Nile. This describes yet another miraculous intervention of God.

Back to Noah. God promises him that He has made provision for the survival of humankind through Noah and his sons, Shem, Ham, and Japheth, along with their wives (see Genesis 6:10; 7:7, 13). Noah was probably still scratching his head because nothing was really making sense. Yet "according to all that God had commanded him, so he did" (Genesis 6:22).

Several times in the Flood narrative, we find that Noah did whatever God asked of him. It reminds us that even when we don't understand the ways of God, we can still believe His Word and walk according to what He has said, not leaning on our own understanding (see Proverbs 3:5, 6).This is a lesson that I will be learning for the rest of my life. The covenant of redemption is a faithful promise God made unilaterally. It means that He chose to save us on His own terms and by Himself, without our help or works. He invites us to accept what He offers us, namely eternal life.

Thus Noah became another link in God's redemption covenant, like Adam, Abraham, Moses, and David.

And the time came to get into the boat.

Get in the boat! Now!

News flash: God is never early, and He is never late (which is another insight I need to keep in mind at all times). The time came for His direct command: "Enter the ark, you and all your household" (Genesis 7:1). Noah stepped into the ark

THE UNIMAGINABLE STORM

without having seen a drop of water! He just believed God's Word: "By *faith* Noah, being warned by God about *things not yet seen*, in reverence prepared an ark for the salvation of his household, by which he condemned the world, and became an heir of the *righteousness which is according to faith*" (Hebrews 11:7; emphasis added).

These eight people (see 1 Peter 3:20) didn't enter alone. No! They took a whole zoo with them into the vessel (you can read about it in Genesis 7:14–16). And when everyone, including Noah, had entered through the door, "the Lord closed it behind him" (verse 16). Noah didn't have the keys to that door. Only God did because *God is sovereign over when the storm starts and when it ends*. OK, that's one more thing I need to remember.

This is how an entire year-long ordeal started for Noah and his family since they would be inside this unusual structure for a bit longer than a full year. The flood came, the unimaginable storm, just as God said it would. And it came from two sources: "the fountains of the great deep burst open, and the floodgates of the sky were opened" (verse 11). It rained for forty days and forty nights until everything was covered with water.

Forty days is an interesting period in the Bible that repeats many times. It usually depicts a period of time when people are challenged to trust God for the way out and not to fear, because He is faithful to keep His promises (forty days of Goliath taunting Israel, forty days of Moses on top of the mountain, forty days of the spies surveying the Promised Land, forty days of Jesus in the wilderness, etc.).

At the end of the forty days, the whole landscape was covered with water. The water took over everything for 150 days. And then God *remembered* Noah.

When God remembers

"But God *remembered* Noah and all the beasts and all the cattle that were with him in the ark; and God caused a wind to pass over the earth, and the water subsided . . . and the water receded steadily from the earth" (Genesis 8:1–3; emphasis added).

In the Bible the verb *to remember* is a covenantal verb; meaning that when God *remembers*, He acts on behalf of His people according to His covenant. It is not that God forgot Noah or that He disregarded His own promises. When God *remembered* His covenant with the people of Israel, He delivered them from their oppression in Egypt (see Exodus 2:24, 25).

Now, when He remembers Noah and all the animals in the ark, God sends a *wind* to pass over the earth (Genesis 8:1). The Hebrew word translated as *wind* in this verse is the same word as *Spirit* in Genesis 1:2 at the beginning of the Creation narrative. This is not a coincidence, for this is a new start for the earth and its inhabitants. The fountains of the deep are now closed, and the rain is restrained (Genesis 8:2), and as the waters recede, "the ark rested upon the mountains of Ararat" (verse 4).

In the next few verses, we find Noah opening the window and trying to find out a bit more about the situation by sending a raven and a dove (see verses 6–12). When the dove did not return to him, Noah removed the covering of the ark, and he saw that the surface of the ground had dried up (verse 13).

Finally!! Woo-hoo! You really have to admire Noah's patience though. Even after seeing evidence of the dry ground, he stayed

THE UNIMAGINABLE STORM

put until God said, "*It's time to leave.*" I am sure, having spent a year in this confined space with all these smelly animals, I would have felt like climbing through the window just to get out! Wouldn't you?

There is a time for everything under the heavens (Ecclesiastes 3:1), and the time had arrived for them to get out of the boat. "Then God spoke to Noah, saying, 'Go out of the ark, you and your wife and your sons and your sons' wives with you. Bring out with you every living thing of all flesh that is with you, birds and animals and every creeping thing that creeps on the earth, that they may breed abundantly on the earth, and be fruitful and multiply on the earth' " (Genesis 8:15–17).

This is definitely re-creation language; the command to "be fruitful and multiply, and fill the earth" (Genesis 1:28), which God had given humans at the very beginning, will be repeated by God to Noah and his sons in Genesis 9:1. It's a new beginning for humanity, and God continues with His original purpose for us. Aren't you happy that God is a God of second chances (and third and fourth, etc.)?

And just like that, Noah and his family found themselves on the other side of the unimaginable storm. All because God was faithful to His covenant to save them.

God's covenant

God's words to Noah that follow are striking: "*I Myself* do establish *My* covenant with you, and with your descendants after you. . . . *I* establish *My* covenant with you; and all flesh shall never again be cut off by the water of the flood, neither shall there again be a flood to destroy the earth" (verses 9–11).

I, Myself, My, I, My . . . God is personally and unilaterally making a covenant with humanity. It is a covenant to save humanity. As I explained earlier, He chooses to save us on His own terms, without our help. We only get to accept and participate in it. The covenant stands on its own without us because it is God's covenant. God gives Noah a sign of His faithfulness to keep His covenant: His bow. Yes, the very same rainbow you see after the rain is the sign of the covenant with Noah; it stands as a symbol of God's covenant mercy.

His way out of the unimaginable storm
There is one more piece of information that I want to offer you before we conclude this first chapter. It is something that took my breath away. The Old Testament, which was written in Hebrew, was translated to Greek about two hundred years before the time of Jesus. This Greek translation (LXX) is used by several New Testament authors when they cite the Old Testament since they also are writing in Greek. All this just to share with you that in the LXX the Greek word for the ark (*kibotos*) of the flood is also the same word used for the ark of the covenant, which was found inside the Most Holy Place in the sanctuary/temple. Blood was sprinkled on top of the ark of the covenant by the High Priest once a year (see Leviticus 16), pointing to God's covenant to redeem the human race through the blood of Jesus at the cross (see Hebrews 9:14). And this takes my breath away!

The truth is that none of us deserve to be saved due to our sinful nature. Sin became an unimaginable storm. And yet God created a way out for us, as He did with the ark of the flood. He came up with a vessel to save us, and we can't add anything to it, nor control it, nor steer it. We can only accept it and get

THE UNIMAGINABLE STORM

into the boat, the boat of the good news of Jesus Christ. He is our way out, and in Him God's covenant of redemption is fulfilled and completed. And if you haven't accepted Him as your Savior yet, do it today. He is our only assurance to get through this world of sin and suffering to the other side: an eternity of peace and joy with Him. Just like Noah, you, too, can become "an heir of the righteousness which is according to faith" (Hebrews 11:7). The way out is all by His grace, and we receive it by faith.

And just as God found a way out for us to be saved, He will also find a way through your current storm, the unimaginable circumstances we face in this life. That is the assurance I have as we traverse through our storm. I am convinced He who has saved us will also find a way for us to get through this particular storm. And that's my story, and I am sticking to it.

2. THE UNTHINKABLE JOURNEY

Unthinkable: (Of a situation or event) Too unlikely or undesirable to be considered a possibility.
—Oxford Dictionary

When a woman discovers she is pregnant, there is an immediate and radical change in her outlook on absolutely everything. All of a sudden everything revolves around the new developing life. I remember it perfectly well. As soon as I knew a baby was coming, I started making changes in my lifestyle. I remember taking long walks because I wanted to be fit for the unborn child to grow healthy and strong. All kinds of wonderful expectations grew in my mind, and happy thoughts warmed my heart. What I didn't ever think was that my pregnancy would last only a short time and that I would have a miscarriage.

If you have lost an unborn baby, as I did, you know the painful emotional roller-coaster ride you undoubtedly go through. When it becomes apparent that you are going to lose the baby, you enter into an unbearable mourning process. In the midst of my sadness, I was told I had to undergo a dilation and curettage procedure to scrape away the uterus lining. The operation was scheduled at a Catholic hospital that was on the provider list of my insurance. I distinctly remember awaiting the inevitable when two nuns entered the waiting room and asked if they could pray with me. I appreciated their compassion and their prayers very much. I still remember it so clearly, even though it was decades ago. The excitement of anticipation mixed with the horrible experience of loss leaves an indelible mark in your heart.

For me the whole process, from the expectation to the loss, took only a short time. But for Abraham and Sarah, it lasted for decades, and the bad news of the imminent loss of the child involved an unbearable journey. Let me tell you the story from the beginning.

The promise
God told Abram:

> "Go forth from your country,
> And from your relatives
> And from your father's house,
> To the land which I will show you;
> And I will make you a great nation" (Genesis 12:1, 2).

And then the specific promise: "To your descendants I will give this land" (verse 7).

Just a side note, Abram was seventy-five years old when he received this call from God to leave his country and this promise of descendants. Just when he was starting to think about retirement, God had a different plan (which He often does).

Three chapters go by, representing several years, and Abram was still childless, a fact that he pointed out to God (Genesis 15:2). That's when God made a promise to him that "one who will come forth from your own body, he shall be your heir" (verse 4). God even used the stars to show Abram how numerous his descendants would be. "And [Abram] believed in the LORD, and He accounted it to him for righteousness" (verse 6, NKJV). This, by the way, is the first explicit biblical mention of what we now call "righteousness by faith," meaning that God declares you righteous in His sight, not by your works but by His grace when you believe His word.*

As you can imagine, the expectation was growing, because when God promises something, surely it will happen. So they waited . . .

The waiting period

Time went by, and they waited and waited. As often happens with us, Sarai, Abram's wife, started to reinterpret God's words, trying to understand what God *really* meant, given that *she* had no child. Perhaps God needed a hand, some help to fulfill His promise. So she made a bold suggestion to Abram: "Why don't you take my Egyptian servant Hagar and make her your second wife, so we have descendants that way" (take a moment to read Genesis 16).

Abram, who we eventually know for his faith, was getting anxious, too, because when days and months go by and nothing happens, we all tend to get anxious. This is how Ishmael was born, which is a whole other story that we will not analyze in this chapter. But let me just say this: When we take matters into our own hands, everyone involved suffers because of our detour. The consequences of our inability to wait on God will often follow us for a long time. And yet God's grace does not abandon us. The angel of the Lord promised Hagar: "I will greatly multiply your descendants so that they will be too many to count" (verse 10). Hagar is the only woman in the whole Bible to receive this type of promise from God.

---

* Righteousness by faith is a foundational Christian doctrine. It is the belief, based on the Bible, that we are declared "right with God" not by our own works but by grace through faith in the One (Jesus) who did all the work.

THE UNTHINKABLE JOURNEY

Meanwhile, God's original plan to give Abram the son of the promise through Sarai did not change. In Genesis 17 God changed the name of Abram to Abraham and declared, "I will make you the father of a multitude of nations" (Genesis 17:5, NET). God changed the name of Sarai as well, even though she was now ninety years old and still barren. "As for Sarai your wife, you shall not call her name Sarai, but Sarah shall be her name. I will bless her, and indeed I will give you a son by her. Then I will bless her, and she shall be a mother of nations" (verses 15, 16).

But Abraham was having a hard time believing what he heard and asked: "Will a child be born to a man one hundred years old? And will Sarah, who is ninety years old, bear a child?" (verse 17).

And God says: "*Absolutely! Sarah will conceive!*" He even gives Abraham the name of the future child, Isaac, and adds: "I will establish My covenant with him for an everlasting covenant for his descendants after him" (verse 19).

Is it clear, Abraham? Can you really believe the promises of the Lord?

How about you? Can you believe in the Lord's promises, even if you have to wait until you are a hundred years old?

The request

As I said earlier, when you are told that you are pregnant, your perspective on life immediately changes. And you can bet that this happened to Sarah. Finally, the son of the promise was born. Wow! Can you imagine their happiness after waiting all those years? God fulfills His promises exactly as He has purposed them, and, by the way, God never needs our help with His promises.

"Now Abraham was one hundred years old when his son Isaac was born to him. Sarah said, 'God has made laughter for me. . . .'

And she said, 'Who would have said to Abraham that Sarah would nurse children? Yet I have borne a son in his old age' " (Genesis 21:5–7).

Can you imagine how elated these elderly parents felt? You can be sure everything changed for them. Max Lucado makes a really funny comment: Sarah became the first woman in history to pay the pediatrician with her Social Security check![1] So funny and yet so true! Who would have thought? Well, God did.

And this is where our main story starts because Abraham could have never imagined the terrible news of the imminent loss of this cherished child for whom they had waited so long. Isaac was the son of the promise, the one through whom God's covenant was going to be fulfilled. They had waited, and now their world was complete. Then Abraham received God's command, "Take now your son, your only son, whom you love, Isaac, and go to the land of Moriah, and offer him there as a burnt offering" (Genesis 22:2).

Wait, what? I can imagine how horrified Abraham was, getting out of his tent and looking up to the stars. *Excuse me? Did I hear it right? Are you really asking me to do this? How can it be? What about Your promise about the stars and the sand?*

Yet the command was unequivocal. It was *that* son, the only son Abraham and Sarah had together. It was Isaac, the son of the promise, whom they loved, who had to be sacrificed. Interestingly this is the first time that the word *love* appears in the Bible because Isaac was indeed the *beloved son*.

At the very beginning of Genesis 22, the reader is given an advantage that Abraham did not have. We are told that this was a test and only a test. But, of course, Abraham did not know that. Why would the God who promised and gave them this son now ask such a thing? And what was Abraham going to do?

THE UNTHINKABLE JOURNEY

The unthinkable journey

God's command didn't make any sense. I am sure Abraham was really wrestling with it—he asked God to reconsider, pleaded for his son, cried, and then asked, pleaded, and cried again. Yet God's order was unambiguous. It included three important verbs that I'd like to highlight because of what happened later: *take*, *go*, and *offer* (Genesis 22:2).

It seems like the story is intentionally told in slow-motion, as we are given every little detail of what Abraham did that morning: he rose early, saddled his donkey, took two young servants and his son Isaac, split the wood, and started the journey (verse 3). Those three days must have been by far the hardest journey of his life, a journey through the desert, both literally and figuratively. On the third day, as he saw the place from a distance, he said something really strange to the two servants accompanying them: "Stay here with the donkey, and I and the lad will go over there; and we will worship and return to you" (verse 5).

Did you notice? *We* will go, *we* will worship, and *we* will return. What was Abraham thinking, using the first-person plural as if he and his son would return together? Was he displaying wishful thinking? Was he in denial?

Well, Hebrews 11:17–19 sheds some light on it: "By faith Abraham, when he was tested, offered up Isaac, and he who had received the promises was offering up his only begotten son; it was he to whom it was said, 'IN ISAAC YOUR DESCENDANTS SHALL BE CALLED.' He considered that God is able to raise people even from the dead, from which he also received him back as a type."

Abraham wasn't only about to offer his son, as horrible as that must feel, but he was going to offer the very son through whom the promise of the covenant was made. So he reasoned that if it actually happened, then God would raise Isaac from the dead. Because God's promises are faithful and true.

We can imagine Abraham climbing that mountain with God's covenant in one hand and the knife in the other—two opposite realities, yet choosing to believe the covenant. God's promises must always trump any other realities we experience. Hang on to those promises, even if it feels like the very promise is dying. It is quite a journey. Often an unthinkable journey. And yet it is one we all, in one way or another, must go through.

The interruption

I can't even begin to imagine how Abraham must have felt on his journey up the mountain, carrying all the tools needed to sacrifice his son—his beloved son. As Abraham was wrestling with God in his soul, Isaac suddenly asked an innocent question that pierced his heart: "Behold, the fire and the wood, but where is the lamb for the burnt offering?" (Genesis 22:7).

Can you imagine? Abraham, who could not make any sense of what was happening, and who did not have any answers yet was hoping and trusting for God to somehow come through, in his confusion and despair blurted out: "God will provide for Himself the lamb for the burnt offering, my son" (verse 8). Little did he know how prophetic his answer would become.

What followed must have been quite blurry and surreal for Abraham as he built the altar, arranged the wood, bound his son (who must have been a willing participant, for he was old enough to escape), and placed him on top of the wood. Then he took the knife in order to take the life of the very son through whom God's promise of his descendants was supposed to be fulfilled. Nothing was making sense, and yet he was sure that

THE UNTHINKABLE JOURNEY

God had required this. He took a deep breath and raised his knife . . . "But the angel of the Lord called to him from heaven and said, 'Abraham, Abraham! . . . Do not stretch out your hand against the lad, and do nothing to him; for now I know that you fear God, since you have not withheld your son, your only son, from Me'" (verses 11, 12).

Wow! What a reversal! Abraham must have hugged his son until he had no more strength left. God had interrupted the slaying, aborted the sacrifice, stopped the knife. Why?

This is where it gets so good that I doubt I have words to explain it. It is exactly when we find ourselves in the darkest hour of the night, when we traverse through the driest deserts and experience the most threatening storms, that God reveals Himself to us in the most profound and unprecedented ways. And that is exactly what happened on that mountaintop.

"Then Abraham raised his eyes and looked, and behold, behind him a ram caught in the thicket by his horns; and Abraham *went* and *took* the ram and *offered* him up for a burnt offering *in the place of his son*" (verse 13; emphasis added).

There is so much here, yet I want to highlight just two extremely important things. First, did you notice the three verbs in italics? *Went*, *took*, and *offered*. The same three verbs that we find in God's command in verse 2: *go*, *take*, and *offer*. So Abraham did completely carry out what God had ordered, yet he did it by offering the ram instead of his son. And that takes us to the other theme of most importance: *in the place of his son* is the first explicit substitutionary statement in the whole Bible. Meaning that a ram took the place of (substituted) the *beloved son*, and God's command was fulfilled. Wow! This amazing substitute that God provided was pointing to an even greater provision of God.

The LORD has provided

"Abraham called the name of that place The LORD Will Provide, as it is said to this day, 'In the mount of the LORD it will be provided' " (verse 14). And in that mount it *was* provided, because Mount Moriah became the city of Jerusalem, outside of which Jesus died (see 2 Chronicles 3:1). In the midst of this unthinkable journey through the desert, God revealed to Abraham how He would send a Substitute prefigured by that ram, Jesus Himself, who would die in the place of each of us. No voice from Heaven was to interrupt the slaying of the Son of God because He was dying *instead of* you and me. Jesus said that Abraham saw His day and rejoiced (see John 8:56), and I am pretty sure the rejoicing happened on top of Mount Moriah. God gave His only begotten, beloved Son in the place of all the sons and daughters. And this profound truth was revealed to the heart of Abraham.

I don't know what challenging place you may find yourself in today. All I know is that God always interrupts our desert journeys with amazing revelations about Himself. He reveals His self-sacrificing love and grace in ways that we can't fully grasp during the good times. I have learned the most about God's love and grace during the unthinkable journeys in my life. And I am pretty sure there are more to come. When you find yourself with God's covenant to save humanity in one hand and a whole different reality in the other, hang on to His promises. He is faithful, He is graceful, and He is loving, even when we don't understand. At the cross He already provided abundantly for our forgiveness and eternal life. Let's trust Him above all else!

---

1. Max Lucado, *The Applause of Heaven* (Nashville, TN: Word Publishing, 1999), 39.

3. THE UNLIKELY PLACE

Unlikely: Not likely to happen . . . improbable.
—Oxford Dictionary

There are things in life, spaces that you never thought you would find yourself in . . . and yet all of a sudden, you wake up, and you are there. That's what happened to me when I found myself outside of a law office, after fourteen years of marriage, about to file for divorce from my first husband. This is not the place to discuss why I had to do this, but I did. I remember staying in the car a bit longer, asking God to communicate with me if I was making a mistake. I asked Him to communicate with me, even to send a written sign with a brick that would shatter my windshield if necessary to get my attention—something obvious, if this was not His will. By then I was already convinced that God has a PhD in communication and has a thousand ways of making sure He conveys what He wants to say.

But what I was not expecting was that during that very difficult season of my life, God would reveal Himself to me in a new and very personal way. One morning, as I was going through the painful process of divorce, I got up and looked out of my second-story window and saw a very thick, impenetrable fog. The fog was so dense that I could see only the tips of the trees above the blanket of fog and nothing else. It was impossible to see through it. And I thought to myself: *This landscape looks exactly like my life right now; I can't see the way, I just can't, and I don't know how to move forward.* Right then and there I felt God speaking to me.

It wasn't an audible voice, just a very clear message in my heart. One that has stayed with me all these years: *Just don't let go of my hand.* That was it. I visualized myself as a little girl walking side by side with Jesus, holding His hand. All I had to do was hold on to His hand because He knew the way, and He would guide me through the fog of my life. Looking out the window of that ordinary room, it became an extraordinary encounter with God that filled me with assurance at an unlikely time.

The visualization was so powerful that I drew it many times since then. I recently bought a painting that now hangs on my bedroom wall of a little girl walking next to Jesus and hanging on to His hand. It was an unlikely place for a promise, an unlikely season for assurance. Yet that was the place and the time when I received this powerful revelation from God that has stayed with me over the years. And even now, whenever I feel lost, I look at that picture to be reminded that the same Jesus still walks with me. And this is exactly what happened to Jacob when he found himself running for his life. He got to a *certain place* and received a revelation and an assurance that he wasn't expecting.

A certain place

Having deceived his father and having stolen the blessing that belonged to his brother Esau, Jacob was running for his life. Jacob had lied, impersonating Esau. He had dressed in Esau's clothing to smell like his brother and covered his arms with fur to fake the hairy arms of Esau so that when Isaac touched him, Isaac would think he was Esau. To make a long story short (which you can read in Genesis 27), after Jacob received the stolen blessing, his brother Esau wanted to kill him. To save Jacob from Esau's wrath, Rebekah tells Jacob that this was a good time to go live

THE UNLIKELY PLACE

somewhere else for a while and to try to find a wife where Jacob's uncle Laban lived in Paddan-aram, which was quite far. And this is how Jacob finds himself in the middle of the desert, alone, afraid for his life, and with a dense fog blanketing his path and his future.

"He came to a *certain place* and spent the night there, because the sun had set; and he took one of the stones of the place and put it under his head, and lay down in that place" (Genesis 28:11; emphasis added).

A *certain place* is a funny way of defining where you are, isn't it? It actually means that this was not a particularly important, holy, or otherwise interesting place. It was of no significance; it was an ordinary place. It just happened to be the place where Jacob found himself when the sun set. Alone and uncertain, he stopped for the night to get some rest. I can't even fathom all that was going through his mind as he tried to quiet down in that lonely, dark, and dangerous place and go to sleep that night. What he didn't know was that this ordinary *certain* place was about to become an extraordinary place in time and space.

> When he lay down to sleep in that unknown spot, many conflicting emotions must have flooded his mind: triumph at securing the family blessing from his virile brother, remorse at having tricked his aging father, relief at being out of range of Esau's anger, apprehension about the long journey ahead to Haran, and a deep sense of loneliness for his mother. God, being aware of Jacob's troubled thoughts and his feelings of vulnerability, knew that this was not the time to condemn Jacob for his acts of trickery. Out of compassion God appeared in order to strengthen Jacob, the

bearer of the promises, for the hard years ahead. He wanted to assure Jacob that the God of his fathers was directing his way in order that the blessings entrusted to his forefathers would be fulfilled through him.[1]

Wow! God knows what we need when we need it, even if we are at a very vulnerable place in our lives. God's compassion and mercy are much greater than our detours. Don't ever forget that.

"He had a dream, and behold, a ladder was set on the earth with its top reaching to heaven; and behold, the angels of God were ascending and descending on it. And behold, the LORD stood above it [or beside him] and said, 'I am the LORD, the God of your father Abraham and the God of Isaac' " (verses 12, 13).

Wait, what? Was God actually communicating with the deceiving, cheating, cunning Jacob to offer him assurance in this *certain place* in the middle of nowhere? Oh, yes! That's my God! Jacob sees a stairway or ramp connecting heaven and earth. Yahweh is there, and God's messengers were going up and down on it. Wow! It's hard to even imagine what Jacob must have felt. Like I said, God has a way of meeting us in the most unlikely places and times. And this is when He reveals Himself in the most unexpected ways. And, as in this case, He makes the most surprising promises.

The surprising promises

All of a sudden Jacob finds himself in a worship experience in the middle of the desert. God reveals Himself as the God of Abraham and Isaac because He has always been a God of people, not a God of places like the pagan gods were. He identifies Himself with Abraham and Isaac and comes to Jacob to offer him the

THE UNLIKELY PLACE

same three-fold covenantal promise that Abraham had received: land, numerous descendants, and a blessing to all the families of the earth through his lineage. "The land on which you lie, I will give it to you and to your descendants. Your descendants will also be like the dust of the earth, and you will spread out to the west and to the east and to the north and to the south; and in you and in your descendants shall all the families of the earth be blessed" (verses 13, 14).

Can you even imagine getting a promise like that when you are at the bottom of your darkest valley and your future is covered by thick fog? Yet that's how merciful God is with us. At that moment Jacob is not even married yet, and he is escaping from his home, his family! Everything looks dark and uncertain. He doesn't have a dime to his name, and yet God is revealing Himself to Jacob and the amazing future of him as a nation through which the Messiah was to come. Wow! These promises must have felt like distant realities to the shame-laden and guilt-stricken Jacob. And yet they were true, just like the promises that God is placing in your heart right now, even though you might feel lonely and undeserving.

As if the Abrahamic covenantal promises were not enough, God goes on to make a four-fold promise about Jacob's immediate future: "Behold, I am with you and will keep you wherever you go, and will bring you back to this land; for I will not leave you until I have done what I have promised you" (verse 15).

Wow! Did you notice the four parts? Look how active God is in Jacob's life! Check out the first-person pronouns; Jacob is the object of all of them: 1) *I am with you*, 2) *I will keep you wherever you go*, 3) *I will bring you back*, and 4) *I will not leave you*. You can even add the last two parts: *until I have done what*

I have promised you. Did you know that when you believe in Jesus, you have the same promises? 1) God is with you, 2) He will keep you, 3) He will bring you back to your original home: paradise, and 4) God will not leave you! He will never abandon you in the middle of your crisis! Woo-hoo! Amazing! Yes, God is meeting you and me here and now, at this very moment, to offer us surprising promises!

"The LORD is in this place"

"Then Jacob awoke from his sleep and said, 'Surely the LORD is in this place, and I did not know it.' He was afraid and said, 'How awesome is this place! This is none other than the house of God and this is the gate of heaven' " (verses 16, 17).

Jacob is amazed that God met him there with a message of assurance. That *certain place* in the middle of nowhere became the house of God simply because God came to be with His boy, Jacob, who was very much in need of some TLC. God always comes to the aid of His children, no matter how dark the detour they find themselves in. And with His presence the ordinary places of our storms and deserts become extraordinary places of praise, worship, and assurance.

It's interesting to me that Jacob says: "*Surely* the LORD is in this place, and *I did not know it*" (verse 16; emphasis added). Somehow, due to our crisis, we often miss the fact that God is with us in the middle of it all. We start wondering if He has forgotten us in our situation or if He doesn't care. I know because I've been there! But as surely as with Jacob, God is with us in our crisis, no matter how dry the wilderness may look to us.

Jacob is so taken by this experience that he decides to create a landmark: "So Jacob rose early in the morning, and took the

THE UNLIKELY PLACE

stone that he had put under his head and set it up as a pillar and poured oil on its top. He called the name of that place Bethel" (verses 18, 19). *Beth-el* means "house of God." It would become an important religious place from that day forward and throughout Israel's history. It was no longer a *certain* place, for it was now a pivotal place where God revealed Himself and made His promises to Jacob.

Then Jacob made a vow: If God would do all that He promised at Bethel, "then the LORD will be my God. This stone, which I have set up as a pillar, will be God's house, and of all that You give me I will surely give a tenth to you" (verses 21, 22).

That "tenth" is usually called *tithe*, and Abraham also practiced it. It is giving back to God a tenth of our income in recognition that all we have comes from Him. We find this practice all over the Bible, and He invites us to try Him on this. I believe this is one of the greatest secrets of financial stability for the children of God because it is tied to a fantastic heavenly promise. Check it out: " 'Bring the whole tithe into the storehouse, so that there may be food in My house, and test Me now in this,' says the LORD of hosts, 'if I will not open for you the windows of heaven and pour out for you a blessing until it overflows' " (Malachi 3:10). This is not the topic of this book, but I just wanted to let you know about it, in case you decide that you want to test God on this. Obviously it worked for both Abraham and Jacob.

Back to Jacob's journey, this story touches me deeply because Jacob didn't deserve anything. He had been a cheater and a con artist. And yet God reached out to him with covenantal promises. So if you ever thought that you went too far . . . well, this story is for you, like it is for me. Just when we think that God doesn't want to have anything to do with us, we realize that there is a Ladder uniting our dark world with heaven and that God is reaching out to us in a very personal and real way. And let me tell you, the ladder is the most important part of the story.

The ladder

It is fascinating to me how the Old Testament stories are developed in the New Testament in light of Jesus' identity and mission. And this story is no exception. In the first chapter of the Gospel of John, Jesus is talking to Nathanael, who would become His disciple, and, in the process, applies this story to Himself: "Truly, truly, I say to you, you will see the heavens opened and the angels of God ascending and descending on the Son of Man" (John 1:51). Here Jesus clearly points to Himself as the true Ladder represented in Genesis 28:12. Jesus is the Ladder that unites heaven and earth, and He is the reason why heaven can reach down to us with the assuring message of His presence in the midst of our crisis, even in our darkest and most confusing moments.

Furthermore, because of Jesus' sacrifice on the cross on our behalf, we are heirs of all the covenantal promises He made to humanity, which we don't deserve yet can be assured of. Jesus took upon Himself the punishment of all our detours, cheating, and betraying, so that we may live without shame and with a bright future for His honor. Therefore, let God meet you in the most unlikely place, in the midst of your crisis, and let Him lavish you with His grace until you, like Jacob, recognize: "Surely the LORD is in this place, and I did not know it" (Genesis 28:16).

---

1. John E. Hartley, *Genesis*, New International Biblical Commentary 1 (Peabody, MA: Hendrickson, 2000), 257.

4. THE UNFAIR PITS

*Unfair: Not based on or behaving according
to the principles of equality and justice.
Unkind, inconsiderate, or unreasonable.*
—Oxford Dictionary

Betrayal is one of the hardest things to experience in this life, especially if you are betrayed by someone very close to you, whom you have trusted with all your heart. I know this kind of pain. Many years ago I was betrayed; and even though I don't want to share the whole story here, the pain I felt at that time was very real. It is part of my life story and, in many ways, it made me who I am today. Back then the betrayal seemed so devastating that it was hard to imagine a future after that. I wish that person well, but I had to leave that relationship if I wanted to preserve my sanity. I could not stay.

During that time I wrote a poem entitled "The Vase." I poured my whole heart into that poem. It talked about how the vase of my life had fallen to the ground and how it had shattered into many pieces. And in the style of the psalms, as the poem progressed, I found hope in the Lord. I wrote about how I was looking at those broken pieces and that I had decided to trust the Master Artisan to put them back together in a way that would make the vase more beautiful and stronger than it was before. And that's exactly what He did. Betrayals throw us into terrible storms. But if we allow Him, God brings us out stronger and wiser than we were before. Our wounds can give Him glory and propel us into our purpose, even when we find ourselves in a deep and unfair pit.

This is where Joseph found himself: inside an unfair pit of despair and loneliness, betrayed by his own brothers and sold into slavery. These types of desert journeys require soul decisions that will change the course of our story. Let me tell you a secret: God is an expert at making sure that *all* things, even the unfair pits, work out for the good of those who love Him, who are willing to allow His redeeming purposes in their lives (see Romans 8:28). So this is the story of a man who chose to believe that God could bring something good out of something bad. Let's start the story from the beginning.

Of dreams and robes
The story of Joseph is the most detailed biography in the first five books of the Bible (Pentateuch/Torah). The story employs a very interesting narrative style with two distinct threads or plots running throughout the story: the robes and the dreams. In the story Joseph wears three different robes that symbolize three different stages of his life. For each of those stages, God sends a set of two dreams. As the story unfolds we see how God turns misfortunes meant for evil into something unimaginably amazing. So let's get started.

The story begins in Genesis 37: "Now Israel loved Joseph more than all his sons, because he was the son of his old age; and he made him a varicolored tunic. His brothers saw that their father loved him more than all his brothers; and so they hated him and could not speak to him on friendly terms" (verses 3, 4).

It's definitely a dysfunctional family, with a favorite son

THE UNFAIR PITS

whose siblings hate him. Now, if you feel a bit above the described situation of dysfunction, think again. In fact there are no perfectly functional families around, not in the Bible, not today. We humans are all dysfunctional. However, God uses us, dysfunctional people, to spread the good news of a Savior because we need one so badly.

In the midst of the dysfunction, the two dreams appear (see verses 6–11). Joseph tells his brothers, "Behold, we were binding sheaves in the field, and lo, my sheaf rose up and also stood erect; and behold, your sheaves gathered around and bowed down to my sheaf" (verse 7). Joseph doesn't seem to have the spiritual gift of interpreting dreams yet, but his brothers interpret the dream for him: "Are you actually going to reign over us? Or are you really going to rule over us?" (verse 8). They hated him even more for his dreams. The second one was similar, and even his father rebuked him for it (see verse 10). Yet no one could have foreseen what was coming around the corner.

The first robe and the first pit

Joseph's brothers went to Shechem to pasture the flocks, and one day Jacob sent Joseph to visit his brothers and report back about their welfare. Yet when Joseph got to Shechem, the brothers with the flocks had moved to Dothan, so he went on to find them there. And you can already imagine how thrilled the brothers were to see him. They said, "Here comes this dreamer!" (verse 19). Their first instinct was to kill him. Wait, what? Crazy, isn't it? Then Reuben, Jacob's firstborn, rescued Joseph from the bloodthirsty brothers, suggesting that they throw him in a pit, an empty cistern.

"So it came about, when Joseph reached his brothers, that they stripped Joseph of his tunic, the varicolored tunic that was on him; and they took him and threw him into the pit. Now the pit was empty, without any water in it" (verses 23, 24).

Pits are places you never thought you would find yourself in. They are sudden, dark, unexplainable, and unfair. I don't know what pit you might be in right now, but I do know that pits are places we don't want to be in.

The brothers sat down to eat a meal as if what they had just done was the most natural thing in the world. They see in the distance a caravan of Ishmaelite traders (or Midianites or Medanites, all descendants of Abraham). The traders were going to Egypt, bringing some special aromatic oils and myrrh.

Judah had an idea: "Let's sell Joseph!" The brothers got twenty shekels of silver for him. That's how Joseph's unfair desert journey started, a journey that would change the course of history. His brothers sold him into slavery! How is that for a dysfunctional family?

Reuben, who for some reason wasn't there with the rest when they sold Joseph, returned to the pit. That's when he found out the horrible news that Joseph wasn't there and wasn't coming back any time soon. He tore his garments in disbelief. But then, instead of telling their father what had happened, they all devised a plan to deceive him.

You know, as disgusting as this sounds, we often do the same, try to cover things up when we realize the consequences of our folly. And yet lies have very short legs. Instead of fixing our problem, we often find that things go a lot worse than they would have if we had immediately confessed our wrongdoings.

"So they took Joseph's tunic, and slaughtered a male goat

THE UNFAIR PITS

and *dipped the tunic in the blood*" (verse 31; emphasis added; please keep this verse in mind, as I will come back to it at the end of the chapter). And that's how the sons of Jacob deceived the deceiver (that's what the name *Jacob* means). I always say that whatever currency you use at home, your children will use with you.

Back to the story—Jacob examines the bloody tunic, obviously Joseph's, and concludes that a wild beast has, in fact, devoured his favorite son. And there was no way of comforting him. "Meanwhile, the Midianites sold [Joseph] in Egypt to Potiphar, Pharaoh's officer, the captain of the bodyguard" (verse 36).

It looks and feels like a terrible detour. And yet the reader is given so much detail about who bought Joseph as a servant, because God is about to turn this around for good. The fact is that Joseph is closer than he has ever been to fulfilling a great purpose of God. But he doesn't know that. Did you know that God is able to turn the most unfair pit into something amazingly fruitful for His kingdom? (See Romans 8:28.)

The second robe and the second pit

"The LORD was with Joseph" (Genesis 39:2). This truth is repeated many times in the story of Joseph. The Lord was with him! But, Lord, he is a slave . . . But, Lord, he is in jail . . . But, Lord, he is away from his family . . . Nevertheless, "the LORD was with Joseph."

There are so many circumstances in life that we don't understand. But one thing we can be sure about, even when we don't comprehend our situation: when we surrender our life to God, He is *with us* every moment.

We are told that "[Joseph's] master saw that the LORD was with him and how the LORD caused all that he did to prosper in his hand. . . . So he left everything he owned in Joseph's charge" (verses 3–6). It was so obvious the Lord was with Joseph that Potiphar made Joseph the overseer over his whole household.

I find it so interesting that all those who would be above Joseph in the hierarchy in Egypt (Potiphar, the chief jailer, and Pharaoh) notice that there is something about Joseph that makes everything he touches prosper, and that it has something to do with his God. As you will find out in a moment, Joseph wore a special robe that identified him as the overseer of Potiphar's household. No one else wore it. Only Joseph did. But not for long.

As it usually happens when everything is looking up, the temptation comes. Potiphar's wife had her eyes on Joseph, and even though he declined her advances over and over, one day she became a lot bolder. Joseph was working in the house by himself with no one else around when she saw an opportunity and "caught him by his garment, saying, 'Lie with me!' And he left his garment in her hand and fled, and went outside" (Genesis 39:12).

Poor Joseph! Every time he gets a new robe, someone strips it off of him! The first garment of Joseph represented the stage of receiving his calling, in the midst of his dysfunctional family. The second robe symbolizes his training through a season of suffering. God doesn't cause bad things to happen to us, yet in His grace He is able to work through suffering and difficult times for our good to cause us to grow, according to His redeeming purposes.

THE UNFAIR PITS

When Potiphar's wife realizes that what she has in her hands is Joseph's identifying robe, she makes a full U-turn, accusing him before Potiphar of rape. Potiphar has no choice but to put Joseph in jail.

If you find yourself in this stage of your life, you need to know that God will train you for the job or ministry He has for you and that your training will have a broader range. Joseph was trained to be an "overseer," first for Potiphar, then in jail, and eventually over all of Egypt. But that wasn't all. He also was trained to develop many important traits of his character, such as patience, integrity, etc. God uses the difficulties and injustices of life to develop those traits in us. Sometimes, even when you do the right thing, you, like Joseph, may end up in jail, but God will use these circumstances to teach you to depend on Him totally.

When in jail, Joseph was put in charge of the whole prison, and that's when another set of two dreams occurred. Remember that each stage of Joseph's life is characterized by one robe and two dreams. God has not lost control over Joseph's life, and He still carries out His purpose for Joseph.

Two of Pharaoh's officers were in jail: the baker and the cupbearer. They had dreams that they couldn't understand, and, for the first time, Joseph is granted discernment to interpret dreams—the cupbearer was going back to work for Pharaoh in three days, but the baker would be hanged.

And here comes one of the most gut-wrenching pleas in all of this story. Joseph speaks to the cupbearer and says, "Only keep me in mind when it goes well with you, and please do me a kindness by mentioning me to Pharaoh and get me out of this house. For I was in fact kidnapped from the land of the

Hebrews, and even here I have done nothing that they should have put me into the *dungeon*" (Genesis 40:14, 15; emphasis added).

The word translated as *dungeon* is the same Hebrew word used earlier in the story when Joseph's brothers put him in the pit, or the cistern (Genesis 37:24). The jail is Joseph's second pit! Joseph must have thought, *Lord, I know that You are with me, but how many pits will You allow me to be thrown into?*

The third robe

There is a detail in the story that I want to highlight. When Potiphar put Joseph in jail, he placed him in the royal jail, where the king's prisoners were confined (see Genesis 39:20). This jail happened to be in the house of the captain of the bodyguard—in other words, in Potiphar's house (Genesis 40:3).

It warms my heart to know that God had directed Joseph's life in such detail that even the person who bought him as a servant in Egypt would be used by God. When Potiphar unjustly placed Joseph in jail, he didn't send him to the regular jail but to the king's jail instead because he was the captain of the bodyguard. The connection between Joseph and the cupbearer would be made in that royal jail, and eventually Joseph would get to Pharaoh through him. I am amazed, humbled, and encouraged by the realization that no detail escapes God's notice, and by His ability to work it for His redeeming purposes.

"Now it happened at the end of two full years that Pharaoh had a dream" (Genesis 41:1). As a matter of fact, he had two dreams. But before we go there, check out the timing: Joseph

THE UNFAIR PITS

spent two more years in jail after the cupbearer went back to Pharaoh, because the cupbearer had actually forgotten Joseph (see Genesis 40:23). God's timing has never, ever matched mine. The sooner we understand that we cannot know what God knows, the sooner we will be able to experience peace.

After two years had passed from the interpretation of the cupbearer's dream, Pharaoh had two dreams that no one could interpret. That's when the cupbearer remembered Joseph. He tells Pharaoh all about Joseph and the interpretation of the dreams (Genesis 41:9–13). Pharaoh immediately sends for Joseph. And this is when another temptation arises for Joseph.

"Pharaoh said to Joseph, 'I have had a dream, but no one can interpret it; and I have heard it said about you, that when you hear a dream you can interpret it' " (verse 15). But Joseph knows that this is not something he himself provides but that it is from God. So he does not hesitate to deflect the attention from himself in order to give glory to God, saying: "It is not in me; God will give Pharaoh a favorable answer" (verse 16). We all need to learn to do the same for God to be able to use us for His redeeming purposes.

Pharaoh told Joseph the two dreams that had troubled his spirit, and Joseph responded that God had told Pharaoh what He was about to do (see verses 25, 28). There would be seven years of abundance and then seven years of great famine, so severe that the years of abundance would be forgotten. Then Joseph gave Pharaoh a word of counsel: "Now let Pharaoh look for a man discerning and wise, and set him over the land of Egypt" (verse 33). He went on to explain how that man would make provisions during the time of abundance for the years of famine.

By now Pharaoh recognizes that Joseph has divine wisdom, because when you submit to God, it becomes obvious that God is with you. "Then Pharaoh said to his servants, 'Can we find a man like this, in whom is a divine spirit?' So Pharaoh said to Joseph, 'Since God has informed you of all this, there is no one so discerning and wise as you are. You shall be over my house, and according to your command all my people shall do homage; only in the throne I will be greater than you. . . . I have set you over all the land of Egypt' " (verses 38–41).

Oh, wow! Who could have imagined what God had planned behind the scenes? And now comes the third robe—remember, for every stage of Joseph's life, there is one robe and two dreams.

"Then Pharaoh took off his signet ring from his hand and put it on Joseph's hand, and *clothed him in garments of fine linen* and put the gold necklace around his neck" (verse 42; emphasis added).

Oh, the robe of the fulfillment of the calling that God had placed on Joseph's life! The breathtaking outcome was in God's hands all along!

You can continue reading the rest of the story, which is fascinating! Joseph organized the provision for Egypt, and when the famine came, they had enough for themselves and to share with others. Marvelously, through this young man, God was able to provide for and preserve Jacob and his descendants, the family line through which the Messiah was to come. Wow! Are you in awe? I am!

The robe dipped in blood

There is another scene at the end of the Bible that I want to

THE UNFAIR PITS

take you to. It's found in Revelation 19. It is a triumphant scene of Christ as Warrior-King. Everything in the scene is white, except One, and the description given reminds us of what we read back in Genesis 37:31. It reads: "And I saw heaven opened, and behold, a white horse, and He who sat on it is called Faithful and True, and in righteousness He judges and wages war. . . . He is clothed with a *robe dipped in blood*, and his name is called The Word of God" (Revelation 19:11–13).

Oh, Jesus' robe is dipped in blood! This time not for deception, as was the first robe of Joseph that his brothers dipped in blood to deceive their father. Oh, no! This time the robe is dipped in blood to remind us of the high price that was paid for our redemption! The blood of the Son of God!

So how do we go through life and the different stages/robes, especially when we find ourselves repeating the cycle of robes and unfair pits? Well, actually, it is quite simple. Whether you find yourself in the first robe, the robe of your calling; or in the second robe, the robe of training and perhaps suffering; or in the third robe, the robe of the fulfillment of your calling, allow yourself to be fully covered by the robe of righteousness of Christ. Only His robe, dipped in blood, assures you of your eternal salvation, and it also gives you three guarantees for the here and now: His Presence, His Provision, and His Purpose for your life. Your eternal salvation is assured in Him, and His Presence, Provision, and Purpose are promises that you can count on in any crisis. Trust the true outcome that God is able to bring out of even the most unfair pits in this life. Take my word for it, I am a walking testimony of His ability to do just that!

5. THE UNYIELDING GIANTS

Unyielding: Unlikely to be swayed; resolute.
—Oxford Dictionary

Have you ever met a giant? I have. And I will never forget it because it was a very, very scary one. I had arrived with great expectations and excitement. While serving as a full-time minister in the United States, I started my distance learning PhD program in the United Kingdom at the University of Gloucestershire. My plan was to travel back and forth as needed. When the day of my study trip arrived, I thought I was ready.

I was on a tight budget, so I had reserved a spot in a youth hostel in Cheltenham. It seemed like a reasonable place to stay. However, when I got there, I realized that this place was totally different from what I had imagined. This was a lodging where troubled young people who didn't have a permanent residence would stay for a night or two. This most definitely wasn't the right place for me, but it was too late to do anything about it. The room was cold, and I felt horrible. I was scared even to head out to the bathroom at night because I wasn't sure what or who I would encounter there. I was hungry, alone, freezing, and uncomfortable. It wasn't anything like I had imagined, and my mind started going down a dark rabbit hole.

The next day was my first meeting with my dissertation supervisor. He was a very kind man and an extremely knowledgeable scholar, known and respected worldwide. He gave me two books to read and said we would meet again in about two weeks. Wait,

THE UNYIELDING GIANTS

what? Am I going to stay like this for two weeks? No way! I can't do this. This is too much. I started to read the two books he had suggested, and they felt like Chinese to me (by the way, I don't know Chinese). Now I was sure this wasn't the place for me.

I started to engage in negative self-talk: *What was I thinking to come to this place! I can't do this! I need to go back and forget this whole venture. It's too much for me!* The giant was too big, too strong, and unyielding. I felt totally unprepared to meet this challenge. Wow! The two weeks were one of the darkest times of my life. I didn't see any way forward. I knew I couldn't do this. I couldn't face this giant.

This is how the people of Israel felt. After their exhilarating deliverance from slavery in Egypt and wandering in the desert for a period of time, they finally arrived at the border of the Promised Land. They were so excited, filled with expectations that had been cherished for hundreds of years. But suddenly their jubilant sentiment was replaced by utter hopelessness when they discovered that there were unyielding giants in the land. They said: "We can't do this. Let's go back to Egypt!"

Do you recognize the feeling? I do. Perhaps you are experiencing something similar right now. Would you join me on a journey to discover that in situations like this, we can choose either to size up the giant's great strength and compare it with our puny muscles, or we can face the giant with the unsurpassed power of our God? We can either panic about the size of our giants, or we can talk to our giants about the size of our God.

The land of grapes and giants

After walking for years on the hot desert sand, the people of Israel were ready for the land of milk and honey. It seems they had requested that Moses send a search team to bring back word about how everything looked in the land they were about to possess (see Deuteronomy 1:22, 23). Spying out the land was a common practice at the time, and the Lord said they should send one man from each tribe. But what I love the most about this is that the Lord gave them the assurance ahead of time: "Send out for yourself men so that they may spy out the land of Canaan, *which I am going to give to the sons of Israel*" (Numbers 13:2; emphasis added).

Did you see that? Wow! It was going to be a gift from God; *He would give it* to them, and it truly was a done deal.

One of the twelve spies was Hoshea, the son of Nun (verse 8). I point this out because I think it is really significant that Moses will change his name from Hoshea to Joshua (verse 16). Joshua would eventually play a great God-appointed role in bringing the people of Israel into the Promised Land.

> So [the spies] went up and spied out the land. . . . When they had gone up into the Negev, they came to Hebron where Ahiman, Sheshai and Talmai, the descendants of Anak were. . . .
>
> Then they came to the valley of Eshcol and from there cut down a branch with a single cluster of grapes; and they carried it on a pole between two men, with some of the pomegranates and figs" (verses 21–23).

Oh, yes! This was definitely a land of abundance! Abundance of grapes, pomegranates, figs . . . and giants! By the way, remember the names of these giants (Ahiman, Sheshai, and Talmai) in case you are looking for a name for your newborn.

THE UNYIELDING GIANTS

Back to our story. It's awesome, isn't it? They have finally arrived at the land they will inhabit, and it is an exceedingly good land! Let's take it! Let's go in! But wait—there's a tiny little problem.

But . . .

"But" is an interesting little word that can introduce either a great victory or a dismal defeat. God loves to incorporate the victorious "buts" in our life stories, as in "I was in a dark hole, *but* God pulled me out." Yet the other type of "buts" are as real, and they work against us. For example, "God had great plans for me, *but* I became afraid and did not pursue them." The latter is the type of "but" we encounter in this section of the story.

"Thus they told him, and said, 'We went in to the land where you sent us; and it certainly does flow with milk and honey, and this is its fruit. *Nevertheless* [but], the people who live in the land are strong, and the cities are fortified and very large; and moreover, we saw the descendants of Anak there' " (verses 27, 28; emphasis added).

Before we get too critical of these people, let's think about ourselves. How many times has this happened to us? The land was a gift from God. They didn't have to wonder about the outcome. When they went to survey it, they found out that, indeed, it was a land of abundance. The fruit was luscious, and everything they had hoped for was there. They were meant to bring back good news of encouragement about the land they were about to possess, *but* they said, "We can't do it—the cities are fortified. There are giants there. We will never conquer it!"

I think it is significant that the spies' surveying period was forty days (see verse 25). There are many references in the Bible to forty days. Yet I also believe that all these forty-days references point to periods of time that will make it evident if the person or group will trust God for their deliverance. There are many examples of forty days: the Flood, Elijah on the way to Horeb, the message of Jonah about Nineveh's destruction, and Jesus in the wilderness, just to name a few.

This story is no exception. The spies found out that this land was exactly as they had been told; *but* the inhabitants were giants, and their cities fortified. So the land was very good, but their chances of conquering the land were very bad—on their own, of course. They forgot their awesome miracle-working God, as we often do.

The Israelites' fear and lack of faith created a reinforcing thought pattern of unbelief that resulted in crazy behaviors. This is important for us to understand. First, they focused on the negative instead of the overwhelmingly positive findings (see verses 27, 28). Then they went on to distort reality, saying that this land "devours" its inhabitants (verse 32). This led them to wish they were dead (Numbers 14:2–4), and ultimately they started blaming God (verse 3), which resulted in their rebellion against Him (verse 4) and, finally, their murderous plans to stone Joshua and Caleb (verse 10). Why did they want to stone them? Oh! Thanks for asking. It was because Joshua and Caleb had a different spirit.

A different spirit

Joshua and Caleb also were experiencing a reinforcing thought pattern, but in the opposite direction. It was a positive one, faith-filled, pointing to God's promises and strength. They started focusing on the positive, highlighting that this was "an exceedingly good land" (Numbers 14:7), and they continued by

THE UNYIELDING GIANTS

describing how God's power would certainly bring them into the land; the outcome was already assured (verse 8)! They went on to remind the congregation that God's presence was with His people. They exhorted them: "do not fear" (verse 9) and be assured. Yet the people chose fear over faith and spoke of stoning these two dissenting voices.

You probably know what happened next, because it has been the theme of many movies and books. The Lord told them the consequences of their unbelief: "According to the number of days which you spied out the land, forty days, for every day you shall bear your guilt a year, even forty years, and you will know My opposition" (verse 34).

Yes, the Israelites would wander in the desert for forty years! Only their children would cross over to the Promised Land (see verses 30, 31). However, there were two exceptions: Joshua and Caleb. The two dissenting voices pleased the Lord, and He made sure both of them got to enjoy the outcome that they had believed from the mouth of the Lord. And all of this because they had a *different spirit*: "My servant Caleb, because *he has had a different spirit* and has followed Me fully, I will bring into the land which he entered, and his descendants shall take possession of it" (verse 24; emphasis added).

Oh, Lord, give us that *different spirit* to believe in Your promises, even when the giants we are facing are intimidating and scary!

But wait till I tell you what happened with Caleb after the forty years in the desert. You would think that Caleb, after wandering for four decades under the scorching desert sun, would have been ready to relax in his new backyard in the Promised Land. Are you kidding? Caleb had a different spirit! Look what he asked for when they finally entered the land of milk and honey:

I was forty years old when Moses the servant of the LORD sent me from Kadesh-barnea to spy out the land, and I brought word back to him as it was in my heart. Nevertheless my brethren who went up with me made the heart of the people melt with fear; but I followed the LORD my God fully. So Moses swore on that day, saying, "Surely the land on which your foot has trodden will be an inheritance to you and to your children forever, because you have followed the LORD my God fully." Now behold, the LORD has let me live, just as He spoke, these forty-five years, from the time that the LORD spoke this word to Moses, when Israel walked in the wilderness; and now behold, I am eighty-five years old today. I am still as strong today as I was in the day Moses sent me; as my strength was then, so my strength is now, for war and for going out and coming in. Now then, give me this hill country about which the LORD spoke on that day, for you heard on that day that Anakim were there, with great fortified cities; perhaps the LORD will be with me, and I will drive them out as the LORD has spoken" (Joshua 14:7–12).

Oh wow! Can you believe it? Caleb asked to inherit the very land were the giants lived. And at the age of eighty-five, he was planning to drive them out. Talk about a different spirit! And Joshua blessed him and gave him that land. And you know what happened? "Caleb drove out from there the three sons of Anak: Sheshai and Ahiman and Talmai, the children of Anak" (Joshua 15:14).

I am speechless! The very same giants that looked so scary to the people of Israel forty years earlier (see Numbers 13:22) were defeated by Caleb himself, at eighty-five years of age! All of this

THE UNYIELDING GIANTS

because he had a different spirit, and the Lord was with him. Amazing and inspiring!

Reminders in the desert

Now let's go back to that pivotal time when Israel did not enter the Promised Land due to their fear of the unyielding giants (the same giants that were eventually conquered by Caleb, an old man, forty-five years later). As we discussed in the previous section, the whole congregation went on to wander in the desert for forty years, one year per day that they had surveyed the land. The Israelites didn't believe that they could conquer it because they didn't believe in the promises of the Lord and His power to do what He said He would do. Now, in the desert, they would learn many valuable lessons about God's faithfulness in keeping His covenant. He sustained them, He provided for them and guided them, He taught them and cared for them. But none of the adults, with the exception of Joshua and Caleb, would enter the Promised Land. The new generation would. And yet they needed to be reminded, once again, not to fear the giants nor the strong nations that they would have to conquer with God's help.

Therefore, Moses exhorted them not to repeat the same mistakes. His reminders are recorded in the book of Deuteronomy:

> "When the LORD your God brings you into the land where you are entering to possess it, and clears away many nations before you . . . seven nations greater and stronger than you, and when the LORD your God delivers them before you and you defeat them, then you shall utterly destroy them.
>
> "The LORD did not set His love on you nor choose you because you were more in number than any of the peoples,

for you were the fewest of all peoples, but because the LORD loved you.

"If you should say in your heart, 'These nations are greater than I; how can I dispossess them?' you shall not be afraid of them; you shall well remember what the LORD your God did to Pharaoh and to all Egypt" (Deuteronomy 7:1–18).

There it is. A great and important reminder for all of us! When you face foes that are greater and stronger than you, when you have to confront problems that look like unyielding giants or end up in situations that are way over your head, do not fear. Simply remember who your God is; remember His power and what He has already done for you, and that He loves you. And then, a second great reminder:

> "Know therefore today that it is the LORD your God who is crossing over before you as a consuming fire. He will destroy them and He will subdue them before you. . . .
>
> "Do not say in your heart when the LORD your God has driven them out before you, 'Because of my righteousness the LORD has brought me in to possess this land.' . . . It is not for your righteousness or for the uprightness of your heart that you are going to possess their land. . . .
>
> "Know, then, it is not because of your righteousness that the LORD your God is giving you this good land to possess, for you are a stubborn people" (Deuteronomy 9:3–7).

The second great reminder, then, is that when God does for us what we can't do for ourselves, we are called to remember that it is not because of our righteousness that He does it. It is not

THE UNYIELDING GIANTS

because we are righteous that we will get to the Promised Land. Oh no! It is *all* God's doing.

It's *all* His doing

Whether we are talking about the giant of salvation (which we can't conquer ourselves) or the giants of the circumstances we face that are stronger than us, the only way to live in peace is to remember that it is *all* God's doing. This was the greatest lesson that Israel failed to remember the first time, and they spent forty years in the desert in order to learn it. When they finally entered the land of milk and honey, they did so under the leadership of Joshua, the leader who succeeded Moses. And I don't think that it is a coincidence that the name *Joshua* (Yahweh saves) is the same name as *Jesus* in Greek. It is the exact same name. And we do well to remember that Jesus has already conquered at the cross. He lived a perfect life in our place, then laid down that life in sacrifice for our sins. He resurrected on the third day and is coming a second time to take us home. It is *done*. It's already conquered. He is the only reason why we will enter the heavenly Promised Land.

So will you choose faith or fear? Will you trust God's way to salvation? Will you trust His power in your daily life? Salvation is by grace through faith. It's *all* His doing. And believe me, no giant is a match for the God of the universe. If you don't believe me, ask Caleb.

Oh! I almost forgot. By God's grace and by His power, providence, and encouragement, I did finish my PhD degree eight years later. Yep! Our God is greater; our God is stronger than *any* giant you may be facing today!

6. THE UNBEARABLE GRIEF

Unbearable: Not able to be endured or tolerated.
—Oxford Dictionary

Grieving is not easy. Mourning a great loss is painful—I remember being there. When my father passed away, a strange and deep sadness took over my soul. I could feel that it wasn't just the sadness of losing my second parent (my mom had passed away two years earlier) but that it was something more.

My friend Hazel sent me an article that helped me find a way through my pain. It explained that when we lose our second parent, there are at least three levels of grieving: First, we mourn both parents again because when the first parent dies, you put all your energy into the parent that is still alive to make sure they are well taken care of. Second, you realize that now you are an orphan, truly without parents. The safety blanket you've had since you were born is gone. And third, you realize that the previous generation is gone, you are next in line, and you become more aware of your own mortality. Well, that article helped me understand the different levels of my grief. Then something happened that took me by surprise.

As I read the Scriptures, different revelations of who God was to me, specifically for that stage of my life, started jumping from the pages. For example, when I read that God is our Father, my mind immediately focused on that aspect of God, and my heart skipped a beat. I was not an orphan after all! My heavenly Father was with me!

THE UNBEARABLE GRIEF

I learned that God reveals Himself to us in personal and amazing ways in the midst of our crises, the storms and deserts of the heart, that are very different from our joyous times. This is why, when I find myself in the middle of a season of pain, grief, or mourning, I feel like taking my shoes off, metaphorically, because I understand that I am on holy ground, in the very presence of God, who wants to reveal Himself to me right then and there.

Are you in a season of unbearable grief? Then this chapter is for you. This is exactly where Naomi and Ruth found themselves, without a path forward or a way out. And it was there that they received something quite unexpected.

Unexpected and unbearable grief

During the time of the judges, before the kingdom of Israel was established, a family decided to cross the desert and the borders of Israel into Moab, looking for a brighter future. There was a great famine in Israel, and they thought they could survive it if they left their hometown of Bethlehem to return when things got better. Just as many of us have done, looking for a better future, the four of them, father, mother, and their two sons, migrated to the other side of the sea. They would live as foreigners in their new home in Moab. But that's when the first unexpected tragedy struck: Elimelech, Naomi's husband, passed away (see Ruth 1:1–3).

Can you imagine having come to another country with great dreams, exciting plans, and expectations and then, all of a sudden, losing your husband?

Naomi and her two sons, living in a foreign land with no family support and no friends, found themselves in such a bitter situation of unbearable grief. The three of them did their best to survive. The two sons married Moabite women. And just when they thought they were going to make it, another wave of unexpected grief struck: the two sons died.

Wow! How terrible! Just when Naomi thought the worst was over, things got a lot worse. In the midst of this tragic crisis, Naomi found herself mourning on many levels: as a wife, as a mother, and as a childless widow with no support and no source of income. She must have questioned if one could ever recover from something like that.

How could God possibly redeem the situation and this unbearable grief? Well, let me tell you what I've learned from the Bible and from my own experience: God specializes in redeeming and transforming our deepest pits and our darkest hours.

Unexpected loyalty

Naomi, childless and husbandless, decided it was time to return to her people. She told her two daughters-in-law, also widows now, to stay in Moab so they could remarry. Her soul was downcast, and you can see how low she really felt when she blamed God for what had happened to her: "The hand of the LORD has gone forth against me" (verse 13).

Has that happened to you, that your grief is so severe that you start blaming God? Sometimes, in crisis, we get confused and start thinking that God is somehow punishing us. Why? We are not sure. Always remember that God loves you more than you can possibly understand and that He is the giver of every perfect gift that His children receive (James 1:17). But I understand that we do get confused due to our pain, because I get confused too.

THE UNBEARABLE GRIEF

Back to our story. Naomi started to say her goodbyes, and one of her daughters-in-law, Orpah, kissed her and went back to her people. But the other, Ruth, uttered the famed words, often used in wedding ceremonies: "Do not urge me to leave you or turn back from following you; for where you go, I will go, and where you lodge, I will lodge. Your people shall be my people, and your God, my God. Where you die, I will die, and there I will be buried. Thus may the LORD do to me, and worse, if anything but death parts you and me" (verses 16, 17).

This was a truly unexpected loyalty. Naomi wasn't alone anymore! God had provided a daughter for her who would walk through the darkness with her. Amazing! But wait! There was much, much more unexpected happiness that God had in store for her, including a fresh revelation of who He is, which would overflow through the centuries until our time. Can't wait to share it with you!

Unexpected provision

The two widows traveled to Bethlehem, Naomi's hometown. Naomi once again crossed the desert between Moab and Israel. I can't imagine how difficult that journey was for them.

The town's women greeted Naomi, saying, "Is this Naomi?" (verse 19). The name *Naomi* means *pleasant* or *sweet*. But she felt so downcast that she wanted to change her name: "She said to them, 'Do not call me Naomi; call me Mara [which means *bitter*], for the Almighty has dealt very bitterly with me' " (verse 20).

If you keep reading, you will find out how empty and afflicted she felt. Have you been there? So burdened, so down that you wanted to change your name to *Bitter*?

Now, they had to survive again. And Ruth, the younger of the two, went out to glean in the fields after the reapers, which was something that poor people did back then for sustenance. "*And she happened to come* to the portion of the field belonging to Boaz, who was of the family of Elimelech" (Ruth 2:3; emphasis added).

What are the chances, right? It was definitely providential! These words highlight God's providence towards her and Naomi.

Ruth found favor in the eyes of Boaz, even though she was a foreigner from Moab. He treated her with kindness and compassion, even commanding his servants to pull out some grain from the bundles for her and leave it for her to glean, so she could get more grain to take home. When Ruth returned home with much more grain than expected, her mother-in-law had questions: " 'Where did you glean today and where did you work? May he who took notice of you be blessed.' So she told her mother-in law with whom she had worked and said, 'The name of the man with whom I worked today is Boaz' " (verse 19). And this is where it gets really, really good.

Naomi started jumping up and down because she knew something that Ruth didn't know, something that could change their lives: the redemption laws in Israel. Frankly, when I understood this, it also changed my life.

Kinsman-Redeemer

If you have followed the Jesus 101 ministry for a while, you know that the kinsman-redeemer *(go'el)* is one of my favorite topics in the whole Bible. At the end of the chapter, I will tell you why it changed my life.

THE UNBEARABLE GRIEF

This is what Naomi knew that Ruth didn't. She said to her daughter-in-law, " 'May he be blessed of the LORD who has not withdrawn his kindness to the living and to the dead.' Again Naomi said to her, 'The man is our *relative*, he is one of our *closest relatives*' " (verse 20; emphasis added).

The word for relative in this verse is *go'el*, which was a big deal in Israel. The *go'el* was the kinsman-redeemer, the closest relative who had several important functions in the family. For example, if a relative were enslaved because of debt, the *go'el* would go and pay their price and set them free. In addition, if the relative had lost property due to debt, the *go'el* could purchase back the property to return it to the original family. The *go'el* was in charge of securing lineage for the family as well as avenging the death of a relative killed unjustly. The *go'el* could even appear in court in the place of a relative.

And that is why Naomi was so excited! Because Boaz wasn't just a source of grain and food for them. No, Boaz could do much more than that! He could redeem Elimelech's property, he could defend their honor, he could marry Ruth, and their children would continue the family line. How exciting that the Lord was providing a *go'el* for them! Naomi interpreted this as God being kind to them (the living and the dead) because this provision was their way out of their unbearable circumstances. Her view of God was changing as her own story was developing.

Let me pause here to remind you that in the midst of the darkest circumstances, God is still with you, and His provision is still secure. This is one of the greatest revelations I got in my darkest pain: God is our utmost Provider, and you can count on that. He provides in every sense of the word: emotionally, financially, spiritually, mentally, and physically. I understand that sometimes grief veils our spiritual eyes, and we start thinking bitterly about God. But if you become convinced that God loves you and that He wants the best for you as soon as possible, you will be able to trust Him, even when you don't understand and your pain seems unbearable.

Back to the story. Naomi did much more than encourage Ruth to continue gleaning in Boaz's field. She started talking with Ruth about future security with Boaz as a husband. Having followed instructions that seem very weird to us today (read Ruth chapter 3), Ruth finally got Boaz's attention and asked him directly to act as their *go'el*, saying, "I am Ruth your maid. So spread your covering over your maid, for you are a close relative [yes, you guessed it—it says *go'el*]" (verse 9). And to make a long story short (please read Ruth chapters 3 and 4), Boaz said yes!

"So Boaz took Ruth, and she became his wife, and he went in to her. And the LORD enabled her to conceive, and she gave birth to a son. Then the women said to Naomi, 'Blessed is the LORD who has not left you without a redeemer [*go'el*] today, and may his name become famous in Israel. May he also be to you a restorer of life and a sustainer of your old age; for your daughter-in-law, who loves you and is better to you than seven sons, has given birth to him'" (Ruth 4:13–15).

Who would have thought that there would be so much happiness after such unbearable grief?

Our *Go'el*

Boaz and Ruth had a son, and his name was Obed. Obed became the grandfather of King David (verse 22). And all of this happened in Bethlehem because God has always worked

THE UNBEARABLE GRIEF

in historical and geographical patterns in the history of Israel so that we wouldn't miss the Messiah when He came to save us. So Ruth married Boaz in Bethlehem, Obed was born in Bethlehem, all of King David's family was from Bethlehem, and Jesus, David's descendant, was born in Bethlehem.

In her darkest pain Naomi found provision from God: First with her daughter-in-law, who, with selfless love, kept Naomi company, took care of her, provided for her, and gave her a grandson, and Naomi became his nanny (see verse 16). Naomi also found a *go'el* who could do for them what they couldn't do for themselves. And I believe you will have the same experience because God will reveal Himself to you as your Provider (as well as many other things) in the midst of your grief, pain, and mourning.

Now to the reason why this topic has changed my life. When God created us in His image (Genesis 1:25, 26), He obligated Himself to rescue us because He is our closest of kin. So the word used in the Old Testament to describe the upcoming Messiah is *go'el*, especially in the book of Isaiah. The word *go'el* is usually translated in our Bibles as *redeemer*, but it means much more than that. Jesus is our Kinsman-Redeemer, our closest relative. He came to fulfill all the functions of the *go'el*: He paid our price and set us free. This is why, at the cross, He said, "It is finished," because the payment for our freedom was complete! He also recovered our property: the earth. And that's why the new earth will be here. He even appears in the heavenly courts in our place. And He fulfills all the other roles of the *go'el*!*

---

* I wrote two books that include a more detailed analysis of the *go'el* topic: *Surprised by Love* (Nampa, ID: Pacific Press®, 2010); *I Will Give You Rest* (Nampa, ID: Pacific Press®, 2015).

This is why I live with the assurance of my salvation—because I have a *Go'el* who has done for me what I could never have done for myself. He has achieved my salvation, and I live with that certainty. Not because my life is perfect but because His life was perfect, and He laid it down for me. He rose from the dead, ascended to heaven, and He is coming back to take us home.

What an amazing provision and reality! This revelation about God truly changed my life, and I trust it will change your life too! Even if you are going through unbearable pain right now, let this truth sink in until you believe it. You have an amazing *Go'el*! God says to you, "Do not be afraid, for I have *go'eled* you, I have called you by name, you are Mine!" (Isaiah 43:1, author's paraphrase).

Amen! Amen! Amen!

7. THE UNDENIABLE CRISIS

Undeniable: Unable to be denied or disputed.
—Oxford Dictionary

I come from Argentina, which, according to the World Health Organization, has the most psychologists per capita in the whole world.[1] But when I was growing up in the 60s and 70s, people within the religious circles didn't talk much about going to therapy. It seemed that the usual counsel for crisis situations was to pray a bit more than before, and that would take care of it. But it's interesting that most people with that kind of mindset would readily go to the doctor when they had physical ailments. I wondered why they wouldn't go to a psychologist or a psychiatrist when they were depressed or not feeling like themselves because of a tragedy or a difficult season.

Things have changed a lot since then. I have personally benefited from seasons of very helpful therapy with Christian psychologists more than once. Looking back, I now recognize that the hardest seasons for me, emotionally and spiritually, occurred after long periods of trying to keep it all together, to pull the cart by myself. And, in some sense, it usually looked like I had been successful. But having lived like that for a number of years with the idea that I had made it, feeling "strong" in the eyes of others, I came to a point of unexpected and surprising discovery. I realized that underneath my facade of strength, I had lingering emotions and pain that would surface at the most unexpected times. That's when I sought (and continue to seek) help from Christian counselors and therapists. I have also learned to trust some of my closest friends and to talk to them when things get out of hand. And this does not make me a bad person or a weak Christian, only a human one.

In the Bible I see that many of the inspiring, strong, and bold characters whom God used powerfully sometimes became quite discouraged in difficult situations. As a matter of fact, they became so disheartened that they no longer wanted to live and actually asked God to let them die. We find examples of such death wishes in the stories of Moses, Job, Jonah, and Elijah, who we will look at in this chapter. These mighty men of God inspire us with their resilience and strength, yet at some point they hit rock bottom so hard that life no longer seemed worth living.

When we contemplate these stories and see God dealing with them with such compassion and tenderness during their dark night of the soul, it has a way of changing something at the core of our being and our view of God. If you can relate to the seasons of pain and desperation described in this chapter, you will find great comfort in knowing how close God is to you when all hope is gone. Even if you are known as a "spiritual giant" who, like Elijah, regularly enjoys mountain-top experiences with fire from heaven—which demonstrate how amazingly powerful your God is—remember that hearing God's gentle voice when you are in the pits is one of the most powerful revelations of who God really is.

The mountain-top experience

If you Google "Mount Carmel Elijah Statue," you will get images of an impressive statue of Elijah, with a sword in hand,

THE UNDENIABLE CRISIS

that greets you when you visit Mount Carmel. It is truly magnificent. It was so amazing for me to be there. The view of the valley beneath took my breath away. Standing there, in the very place where God answered Elijah's prayer with fire from heaven, is quite an emotional and spiritual experience. It is a "woo-hoo!" moment of awareness about God's power and faithfulness that fills you with awe. You can read this inspiring narrative in 1 Kings 18:20–46.

Elijah is the intrepid prophet who defies the 450 prophets of Baal and the people of Israel, saying: "How long will you hesitate between two opinions? If the Lord is God, follow Him; but if Baal, follow him" (verse 21). Tucked in the next verse, almost unnoticed, is Elijah's belief that he is the only prophet left, the last man standing in honor of God: "I alone am left a prophet of the Lord, but Baal's prophets are 450 men" (verse 22). This is a worldview that sounds like trouble.

Please take a moment to read the whole story of the mountain-top experience that culminates in an incredible showdown with fire from heaven at Elijah's request, and God's prophet killing the 450 false prophets of Baal by the brook of Kishon (verse 40). Frankly, this story smacks a bit like a biblical Rambo. This is the ultimate picture of a strong prophet if we ever saw one! Furthermore it seems that, finally, the people of Israel saw the light, because their response to the heaven-sent fire was, "The Lord, He is God; the Lord, He is God" (verse 39). And if that's not enough to give you a spiritual high, right after the Mount Carmel experience, Elijah prays, and God sends rain, ending the three years of drought that had been the result of their unbelief.

So if you were Elijah, this was probably the most successful day of your career or ministry, a kind of life-achievement-award-winning day. Everything you stood for, during all those years of being hunted down by an unbelieving king, now proves to be right. Everyone witnesses the fire from heaven, manifesting, without a doubt, that all along you had been on the right path and on the right side of the divide. So now that you know without a shadow of a doubt that God is with you, you will be above all mundane and petty circumstances of life, right? Well, not so fast. God is with you all right, and He will never leave you for sure, but the human heart is frail, and fear can easily take over. It has a way of overwhelming your mind and heart even within five minutes of witnessing the hand of God in your life.

Overwhelming discouragement

I am so thankful that the Bible contains not only chapter 18 but also chapter 19 of 1 Kings, lest we've got the wrong impression that true Christians dwell on mountaintops only. They don't. There are valleys between the mountaintops, and even prophets and "spiritual giants" get overcome by fear and discouragement when they don't see a way out of their valley.

"Now Ahab told Jezebel all that Elijah had done, and how he had killed all the prophets with the sword. Then Jezebel sent a messenger to Elijah, saying, 'So may the gods do to me and even more, if I do not make your life as the life of one of them by tomorrow about this time.' *And he was afraid, and arose and ran for his life* and came to Beersheba, which belongs to Judah, and left his servant there" (1 Kings 19:1–3; emphasis added).

Wait, what? Could this be the same guy who, a moment earlier, had been as bold as it gets, fearlessly defending God's honor? Could this be the same prophet who, five minutes earlier, had killed 450 idol worshipers? Is he now terrified of one woman? What's going on?

There must be something else going on here than just fear of Jezebel's death threat, because Elijah had received plenty of those before. Plus, he couldn't have been particularly afraid of dying, as a moment later, he would ask God to let him die. The real issue was that he was utterly disappointed. Elijah probably had hoped that what had happened on Mount Carmel would start a great reform, not only for the people but also for the king and queen. He must have surely thought such a powerful manifestation of the supremacy of the God of Israel would create a swift and decisive spiritual reform, and they would turn from Baal to the true God. But when that didn't happen, the prophet felt that his ministry was good for nothing, that his efforts had been wasted with no tangible results. He became disappointed, discouraged, and depressed (the three D's). He traveled to Beersheba, the farthest town to the south within the territory of God's people, bade his servant goodbye, and went on a day's journey into the wilderness.

I find DeVries's commentary helpful to understand what might have been going on in the mind of the prophet Elijah:

"The point is that Elijah interprets Jezebel's personal attack on him as the end of his ministry. The prophet's dismissal of his servant at Beersheba, the southernmost limit of Yahweh's land, signifies that he is abandoning it altogether. A day's journey into the Negeb is as far as he intends to go; he lies down weary unto death and prays for Yahweh to let it be enough; his forefathers are in their graves, let him be as they are, for he is no better than they (v 4)."[2]

In the wilderness Elijah sat under a tree and asked God to let him die: "But he himself went a day's journey into the wilderness, and came and sat down under a juniper tree; and he requested for himself that he might die, and said, 'It is enough; now, O Lord, take my life, for I am not better than my fathers' " (verse 4). Plain and simple. He was done with life, with ministry, and with trying to make a change; he was done with everything.

Can you relate? I certainly can. But just like us, what Elijah didn't realize at the moment of despair was the fact that God's love is stronger than our discouragements, and His grace is greater than our failures and detours. His mercies are new every day, and His compassion reaches down into our darkest pits to lift us up.

God's undeniable compassion

"He lay down and slept under a juniper tree; and behold, there was an angel touching him, and he said to him, 'Arise, eat.' Then he looked and behold, there was at his head a bread cake baked on hot stones, and a jar of water. So he ate and drank and lay down again" (verses 5, 6).

Wait a minute! Did God bake for him? Really? Don't you love it? Instead of scolding him or telling him that weak prophets don't have a place in His kingdom, God sent His angel to gently touch him to wake him up so he could eat divinely prepared food, drink some water, and sleep a little more. I am so moved by this scene. God did not abandon His child when he fell into a dark hole of depression and anxiety. No way! And He doesn't abandon us either.

"Did God forsake Elijah in his hour of trial? Oh, no! He

THE UNDENIABLE CRISIS

loved His servant no less when Elijah felt himself forsaken of God and man than when, in answer to his prayer, fire flashed from heaven and illuminated the mountaintop. And now, as Elijah slept, a soft touch and a pleasant voice awoke him."[3]

Oh, wow! Did you let that statement enter into the core of your soul? God loved Elijah no less in the pit of discouragement than when he was standing by the altar calling down fire from heaven! Woo-hoo! God loves you the same in the darkness of your porn addiction and in the middle of your vomit when you are drunk as He does when you are praying with your neighbor and praising God at church. His love for you is not subject to your circumstances or feelings. God *is* love. That's who He is. And He loves all, all the time.

After Elijah ate the bread cake and drank the water, he fell asleep again. He was not only down, he was totally exhausted. The angel of the Lord came back a second time, woke him up, and said something that touches my heart: "Arise, eat, *because the journey is too great for you*" (verse 7; emphasis added).

God's compassion moves me for many reasons, especially when He tells me, "*This journey is too great for you.*" There are some journeys that are too great for us. I know because I am on one of those right now with my husband's long-term illness. We make tons of mistakes in the process, and still God does not abandon us because of His love and grace and because He knows our human frailty.

So Elijah got up and ate and drank again, then he took a hike of forty days from the strength of that celestial meal. Looking for a fresh revelation of the God he had served all those years, he went to meet Him on a very special mountain.

Even if you are a preacher or a minister, sometimes you

will have to face a crisis big enough to require a new and fresh revelation of God for yourself.

God's unexpected revelation

After forty days and forty nights, which, as we mentioned before, is a very significant period of time in the Bible that denotes an opportunity to trust God for a way out, Elijah finally arrived at Horeb, the mountain of God. This was the very place where, hundreds of years earlier, God met Moses, speaking to him from a burning bush (see Exodus 3:1, 2). No doubt Elijah was looking for a burning-bush experience, an extraordinary word from God. He got into a cave, and the first thing he heard from God was a question: "What are you doing here, Elijah?" (1 Kings 19:9).

In one mouth-full, as if sitting on the sofa of a psychologist, Elijah spilled out everything he was feeling from the bottom of his heart: "I have been very zealous for the LORD, the God of hosts; for the sons of Israel have forsaken Your covenant, torn down Your altars and killed Your prophets with the sword. And I alone am left; and they seek my life, to take it away" (verse 10).

Oh wow! How is that for a confession? Elijah felt alone and completely abandoned. Plus, it seemed like his ministry had no positive effect on the spiritual life of Israel. So why go on? Nothing was working!

Yet God interrupted his pity party and told him to stand in front of the Lord. And this fire-from-heaven type of prophet found himself in a powerful, rock-shattering type of wind. Surely God must have been in this kind of wind, with His power and might blowing the prophet's socks off, right? Wrong!

"The LORD was not in the wind" (verse 11). Then an earthquake hit, but God wasn't in the earthquake either (verse 11). Then a fire! Certainly God would show up in the fire, like the one on Mount Carmel. Plus, don't forget that Elijah was a fire-and-brimstone type of a prophet. Imagine his surprise when he discovered that God was not even in that fire (verse 12)!

After all these powerful manifestations of nature, there was like a sound of a whisper in a gentle breeze. "When Elijah heard it, he wrapped his face in his mantle and went out and stood in the entrance of the cave. And behold, a voice came to him and said, 'What are you doing here, Elijah?' " (verse 13). Elijah was so used to the thunderous manifestations of God's power that he would have never guessed God could show up in a tender small voice.

When we are down in the pits, God always comes softly, revealing His presence, not in the fire-and-brimstone type of sermons but in a gentle breeze blowing on our face, touching our soul, and bringing healing on its wings. That's my God! Gentle with the confused and disheartened. Gentle with me in my questionings and frustrations. "A bruised reed He will not break, and a dimly burning wick He will not extinguish" (Isaiah 42:3). He is, and will always be, on the side of the weak! Don't you love Him for it?

Elijah answered exactly the same way as before. Poor guy, he really believed that he was the only one left and that his ministry had been good for nothing (see verse 14). And, once again, God did not join his pity party. Instead God revealed to him that He was not done with him and still had great plans for him: he would be anointing a new generation of kings and a prophet to succeed him. Furthermore God revealed that

Elijah was by far not the only faithful one left: "Yet I will leave 7,000 in Israel, all the knees that have not bowed to Baal and every mouth that has not kissed him" (verse 18).

Elijah was to leave a great legacy, one that we still talk about, as we are doing in this book. And, by the way, Elijah was one of the few humans in history who went to heaven without tasting death. But, while he was under that juniper tree contemplating suicide, there was no way he could have imagined what God had planned for his future. Neither can you. Neither can I.

Let's quiet down our hearts long enough to hear His gentle voice, whether we are on the top of a mountain, in a valley, or in a cave.

Another mountain

One thing Elijah could not have possibly imagined was that there was one more mountain-top experience waiting for him in the far, far future. As I mentioned previously, Elijah was taken to heaven without tasting death. You can read all about it in 2 Kings 2. Yet, after his ascension, he still had one more mission to fulfill on earth.

Hundreds of years after the events described in this chapter, Jesus was about to give up His perfect life in sacrifice for our sins. He was about to die a criminal's death on a cross, all because He loves us with an infinite love, and His compassion is greater than our sins. But before He went to the cross, Elijah and Moses were sent from heaven to encourage Jesus. And if there was anyone who, from personal experience, could identify with someone needing encouragement, it was Elijah.

"And while [Jesus] was praying, the appearance of His face became different, and His clothing became white and

THE UNDENIABLE CRISIS

gleaming. And behold, two men were talking with Him; and they were Moses and Elijah, who appearing in glory, were speaking of His departure which He was about to accomplish at Jerusalem" (Luke 9:29–31).

Wow! I am speechless! These two men of God, who each at one point in their lives had asked God to let them die because of their discouragement with their ministries, were summoned to miraculously show up on the Mount of Transfiguration to encourage Jesus before His death on our behalf. They could understand what it was like to face what seemed like an insurmountable task. Jesus was about to attempt the greatest rescue of all time: the salvation of the human race. And who could be better qualified to offer encouragement and perspective in such a time as this? Elijah was one of the two chosen.

Only Luke tells us what the three of them talked about. They were talking about Jesus' upcoming death (see verse 31). Elijah had stared death in the face and learned that God speaks to us differently when we can't see a way out. And, in this case, God sent Elijah to carry out the task. Wow! I wonder if God has a similar ministry for you—to encourage others in the same area where you needed encouragement the most.

In the stage I am in, I need to remember this story often. When we can't see a way out, God reveals Himself, and He does it compassionately, not with fire and brimstone. He comes to whisper His grace, His love, and the fact that He has not abandoned us. He often bakes "bread cakes" for us, moments of tenderness designed to encourage us. Because He lived, died, and rose for us, we can live with the assurance of eternal salvation and with the certainty of His presence and purpose for us, here and now.

I have heard it said that your current *test* might become your greatest *test*imony, and your present dis*appointment* might turn into the best *appointment* with God. Elijah would agree. Be encouraged, my friend. The eternal God is at your side, no matter how dark the valley you find yourself in.

---

1. Lucila Sigal, "Sick Again, Argentine's Economy Eats Away at Nation's Mental Health -Study," Reuters, August 10, 2022, https://www.reuters.com/world/americas/sick-again-argentines-economy-eats-away-nations-mental-health-study-2022-08-10/.

2. Simon J. Devries, *1 Kings*, 2nd ed., Word Biblical Commentary 12 (Grand Rapids, MI: Zondervan, 2004), 235.

3. Ellen G. White, *Prophets and Kings* (Mountain View, CA: Pacific Press®, 1917), 166.

8. THE UNEXPECTED WILDERNESS

Unexpected: Not expected, nor regarded as likely to happen. Unforeseen. Unanticipated.
—Oxford Dictionary

I don't like in-between times. These are the times when you have already left point A but have not yet arrived at point B, and you might not even know what point B looks like! All you know is that the in-between, the gap or space between the two points, looks nothing like you had imagined it to be.

I've had numerous in-between periods in my life, many of which you already know because I have already shared them in this book. For example, the time between my divorce and the second marriage, the time between starting and completing my PhD, or the time between the cancer diagnosis for each of my parents and their passing. I still remember the in-between period (years, actually) of waiting to change my immigration status from student to legal resident of the United States. The in-between time of a pregnancy, from conception to birth (which in my case didn't end in the happy delivery that I was hoping for). And right now I am in the middle of yet another in-between time: from my husband's diagnosis several years ago and the slow neurological decline toward the inevitable end of his life. And I could mention many more.

The truth is that I really don't like the in-between times. It has been said that faith is not leaving point A to go to point B. It's just leaving point A. And I get it. I have no doubt that in-between times are faith-building, and God reveals Himself to us in marvelous ways during those times. I am a witness of that. And yet I also know from experience that these periods usually take us by complete surprise—they are unexpected and unplanned. And most of the time, they are much longer than anticipated.

David found himself in one of these unwanted in-between times when, after being anointed king, he had to run for his life. He was trying to escape from a crazy king who decided to kill him because he felt threatened by David's divinely appointed success. And yes, it was unexpected, unplanned, and longer than anticipated.

Between the anointing and the appointing

I remember this phrase from Alyssa Foll, a fellow preacher, who said in one of her talks: "Between the anointing and the appointing." This phrase has stayed with me all these years, perhaps because I am not a very good friend of in-between times. And I am quite sure that David would agree with me because there was quite a bit that happened in his life between his anointing and his eventual appointing as king.

After being anointed king by the prophet Samuel (see 1 Samuel 16), "the Spirit of the LORD came mightily upon David from that day forward" (verse 13) to enable him to do the task for which he was chosen. The next chapter in the Bible (1 Samuel 17) narrates the well-known confrontation between Goliath and David. As you know, God delivered an astounding victory for Israel through this young shepherd who would be king. Therefore we expect the following chapters in David's life to be one victory after another, given that he was being

THE UNEXPECTED WILDERNESS

prepared to lead God's people. But that is not what happened.

King Saul turned against David and started mistreating and persecuting him for no apparent reason other than his jealousy. David found himself in an unexpected desert of the soul. He now was enrolled in the school of brokenness, the same school where many of us have come to know God better, even though we don't understand what is going on or why God is allowing certain things in our lives.*

I was very blessed by a book entitled *A Tale of Three Kings*, by Gene Edwards. The author proposes that God used Saul to kill the *Saul* in David so that when David became king, he wouldn't be like Saul.[1] Please take a moment to re-read that last sentence. It is so profound! This experience for David was like enrolling in a class in the school of brokenness. The same happens to us in our desert experiences. As much as I dislike these classes, I must admit that "Desert 101" has taught me, and continues to teach me, much about God's mercy and grace.

In just a few verses, we learn that, during this time, David was dwelling in the wilderness and the strongholds he found in the desert. Among the places mentioned, we find the cave of Adullam (1 Samuel 22:1) and the strongholds of Engedi (1 Samuel 23:29).

I was very fortunate to get to visit the wilderness of Engedi. As I stood there, in awe of the majestic natural strongholds and caves, I kept thinking of this young man who found himself not only in a physical desert but also in a spiritual desert, or wilderness, of the soul. That is a place where we live suspended

---

* For a detailed study of the life of David, see my book *After God's Heart: A Study in Brokenness From the Life of David* (Nampa, ID: Pacific Press®, 2017).

in a question mark: *What is going on? Isn't God leading me? Didn't He choose me for something special? I am not sure I can survive this!*

The desert of the soul

Over the years I've repeatedly shared my conviction that when all you have left is God, you come to the realization that God is more than enough. And that is so very true. It doesn't mean that you won't have moments of anxiety or desperation when you can't see the end of the tunnel, or even wonder if God's GPS is broken. The desert of the soul is a place where we encounter God in a very personal and intimate way. Usually, at a place like this, we have no answers, just questions.

I find myself there right now as I write this book. But it is not my first trial, so I trust God to see me through, just as He has done before. That doesn't mean that I am immune to feeling sad, anxious, or even desperate at times. I know there are people out there who think they are super-Christians, who claim we should never have these feelings. I disagree. It is part of being human, even if you are a believer. Even Jesus cried out to God, "WHY HAVE YOU FORSAKEN ME?" (Matthew 27:46). We will return to this topic at the end of this chapter.

The wilderness of the soul is a spiritual cocoon, a place where we grow our wings. I have always been fascinated by the fact that the cocoon is both a tomb and a womb—a tomb to the caterpillar and a womb to the butterfly. It is a place where we wrestle with God because we feel as if we are dying, and yet, at the same time, we are being reborn. David was there, learning about God and himself in the middle of the desert.

It was during that time that David learned to extend grace

THE UNEXPECTED WILDERNESS

and be compassionate. First, he started leading a band of misfits: "Everyone who was in distress, and everyone who was in debt, and everyone who was discontented gathered to him; and he became captain over them. Now there were about four hundred men with him" (1 Samuel 22:2).

Wow! Can you imagine yourself leading this type of group? Four hundred distressed, downtrodden, and discontented people. How is that for an introduction to leadership?

Eventually David's band grew to six hundred, and they went through a lot together. During this time David also learned to treat his enemies with grace and compassion, starting with the crazy King Saul, driven by jealousy to a murderous headhunt.

Saul and his three thousand men were pursuing David. Saul needed to go to the bathroom and retreated into a cave without realizing that inside that cave were David and all his men. They must have been very quiet because Saul, having done his business, left. He did this without realizing that David, instead of killing him, had cut off the edge of his kingly robe. When David showed it to Saul from a distance, Saul wept and went home—at least for a little while before going after David, *again*. Take a moment to read this whole fascinating (and somewhat amusing) story in 1 Samuel 24.

The question is obvious: Why didn't David just kill Saul when he had the chance, even if Saul was the anointed king at the time? Great question! David not only was learning grace and compassion toward the undeserving ones, but he also was learning to wait on God to unfold His will in His own timing. This is a lesson that I need to learn over and over again because I am not very good at it. Oh, and there was one more thing that David was learning in the desert.

Teaching your heart to sing in the dark

One of my favorite authors, Ellen G. White, talks about how some birds are trained to sing a special song. When I read this for the first time, it made a real impact on my mind. It goes like this:

> In the full light of day, and in hearing of the music of other voices, the caged bird will not sing the song that his master seeks to teach him. He learns a snatch of this, a trill of that, but never a separate and entire melody. But the master covers the cage, and places it where the bird will listen to the one song he is to sing. In the dark, he tries and tries again to sing that song until it is learned, and he breaks forth in perfect melody. Then the bird is brought forth, and ever after he can sing that song in the light. Thus God deals with His children. He has a song to teach us, and when we have learned it amid the shadows of affliction we can sing it ever afterward.[2]

Wow! Does it mean there are melodies our hearts can learn only in the wilderness? I know this to be true from my personal experiences. I don't believe God sends terrible things to His children. But I do believe He uses difficult times to mold us in the light of who He is and in the amazing love and grace He has for us. There have been revelations of God that I could receive only as I was struggling, wrestling with Him, wondering if He had forgotten me in a dry land. God continues to reveal Himself to me in the midst of my deserts and questionings. That's what happened to David.

During his in-between time in the wilderness, David wrote

THE UNEXPECTED WILDERNESS

beautiful prayers, songs, and poems that are still with us today. At the beginning of some of the psalms David wrote, there is a description of the circumstances he was in when he wrote them. For example, Psalm 142 reads, "When he was in the cave. A prayer," and Psalm 57 reads, "When he fled from Saul in the cave." Take a moment to read these psalms; I find them fascinating.

I started writing my own prayers too. Some are praises, some are laments, and some are requests for mercy and deliverance. But somehow, through this process, I always receive the same assurance from God: "*I am with you, and I will never leave you.*"

David had been *anointed* king, but he had not yet been *appointed* king. His heart was being molded to beat in unison with God's heart, and that lesson could only be learned in the wilderness.

Keep talking with God in the darkness. Write psalms and prayers; communicate with Him about what is weighing on your heart. You will never ever forget what you learned about Him in the darkness. In the midst of affliction, you will find that God is truly a refuge, a present help when you are frightened: "When I am afraid, I will put my trust in You" (Psalm 56:3).

My God, my Refuge

Having gone through several desert experiences, David was finally appointed king (see 2 Samuel 5). He received a covenant from God that one of his descendants would have an eternal reign (2 Samuel 7; Jeremiah 33:17). Jesus was that Davidic King whose kingdom will never end.

Everything about David's life was extraordinary. Yet, for me, one of the most important stages in David's amazing life was the wilderness time that preceded the kingdom. When I stood in the desert of Engedi, with its strongholds and natural fortresses, I could better understand the visualizations David used in his songs and prayers, such as Psalm 144:

Blessed be the LORD my rock, . . .
. . . my fortress,
My stronghold and my deliverer,
My shield and He in whom I take refuge" (verses 1, 2).

Everything around me looked like fortresses or strongholds! David was applying these as metaphors for who God was in his life, using the first-person singular possessive pronoun: *my* refuge, *my* fortress. In the wilderness of the soul, God becomes extremely real and personal. I want to join David in declaring that God is *my* refuge, even when I don't see a way out, or when I don't understand what He is allowing in my life.

In addition, I find great comfort in something Jesus did when going through His in-between time on the cross. Feeling separated from His Father, Jesus uttered the words from Psalm 22:1, a psalm of David: "*MY* GOD, *MY* GOD, WHY HAVE YOU FORSAKEN ME?" (Matthew 27:46; emphasis added).

Even though Jesus was feeling forsaken, like David, He still used the possessive pronoun: *My.* He was not going to let go of *His* Father, even though He felt surrounded by a darkness greater than any of us will ever experience. He felt forsaken in my place so that I may never be forsaken by God, despite my sinful nature and detours. And this is why I am assured of my salvation. If you choose Jesus, nothing will be able to separate you from His love (Romans 8:38, 39). Nothing!

THE UNEXPECTED WILDERNESS

Are you feeling exhausted in your in-between time? Let *your* God be *your* refuge and strength. He will reveal Himself to you as Sustainer, Provider, Redeemer, and Lover of your soul. And while you wait on Him, let Him teach you to sing from the heart—after God's own heart.

> I waited patiently for the LORD;
>   he turned to me and heard my cry.
> He lifted me out of the slimy pit,
>   out of the mud and mire;
> he set my feet on a rock
>   and gave me a firm place to stand.
> *He put a new song in my mouth,*
>   *a hymn of praise to our God.*
> Many will see and fear the LORD
>   and put their trust in him (Psalm 40:1–3, NIV; emphasis added).

---

1. Gene Edwards, *A Tale of Three Kings: A Study in Brokenness* (Wheaton, IL: Tyndale, 1992), 9.
2. Ellen G. White, *The Ministry of Healing* (Mountain View, CA: Pacific Press, 1905), 472.

9. THE UNNERVING DETOUR

*Unnerving: Causing one to lose courage
or confidence; disconcerting.*
—Oxford Dictionary

Like anyone else, I have made a few major mistakes, taken detours that were my responsibility, and fallen into my share of self-inflicted and life-altering pits. As I am settling into my sixties, I look back to thank God that His grace is sufficient to cover my past, present, and future mishaps. And I have come to understand that wholeness comes to our souls when we accept those areas in our lives that were not kosher and turn them over for God to cover them with His amazing grace.

> I am that to which I gave short shrift and that to which I attended. I am my descents into darkness and my rising again into the light, my betrayals and my fidelities, my failures and my successes. I am my ignorance and my insight, my doubts and my convictions, my fears and my hopes. Wholeness does not mean perfection—it means embracing brokenness as an integral part of life. I'm grateful for this truth as age leads me to look back on the zigzagging, up-and-down path I've hacked out during my far-from-perfect life.[1]

Yes, that says it all.

During my youth one of my mistakes ended up becoming life-threatening and landed me in a situation that I should have

THE UNNERVING DETOUR

never been in. There is no benefit in giving too many details here, but I want to let you know, from my own experience, that nothing in our lives is beyond God's ability to redeem. Nothing. And I don't even want to list the things you might be thinking about in your life, because it could be endless. Yet I am convinced that, even if you were Hitler himself, you are not beyond God's forgiveness when you allow His grace to reach you.

Over four decades ago this dark detour landed me in a serious situation. I remember being on a bus from one state to the other, fearing that I could die in the next few hours or days. And yet this was one of the main spots where I found God's grace, in spite of the fact that I didn't deserve it. I believe this is one of the main events in my life that would later result in me becoming an unashamed preacher of the gospel, because I am the recipient of so much of God's grace.

This was an episode in my life that I compare with Jonah's encounter with his graceful God inside the belly of the fish. But let's start our story with the storm that landed him there.

The unquenchable storm

I am sure you've heard the story of Jonah, simply because it is one of the most popular children's stories and one loved by many cartoon production companies. I hope you have already identified a deep and dark detour in your own life to which you can apply this story, especially if you landed in a regrettable place like me due to your own folly.

It all started when God called His prophet Jonah to go tell the Ninevites that grace was available to them if they decided to repent before God's judgment fell on them. But, because the Assyrian Empire—of which Ninevah became the capital—had been bothering the Northern Kingdom of Israel for quite a while, this judgment prophet didn't want them to be the recipients of God's grace. In Jonah's eyes they deserved the punishment, so he wouldn't be the herald of possible good news for them. No, sir! So he found a ship going to the furthest place in the opposite direction: Tarshish (see Jonah 1:3). That's where he was heading, running away from the place God wanted him to go. Sound familiar?

"The Lord hurled a great wind on the sea and there was a great storm on the sea so that the ship was about to break up" (verse 4). It was such a mega storm that even the sailors, in their fear, replaced their usual cursing with prayers, each crying out to their god (verse 5). Jonah, who was asleep through it all, got a wake-up call from the captain to pray to whatever God he believed in to see if something or Someone could help in their dire situation (verse 6). The men decided to cast lots to see if anyone should be responsible for the mysterious calamity. And guess what? It fell on Jonah! There were many questions asked of Jonah, but he cut to the chase and told them what was going on.

> He said to them, "I am a Hebrew, and I fear the Lord God of heaven who made the sea and the dry land."
> Then the men became extremely frightened and they said to him, "How could you do this?" For the men knew that he was fleeing from the presence of the Lord, because he had told them (verses 9, 10).

You see, the fact that you have taken a tremendous detour doesn't mean that you no longer believe in your God. It may mean many other things: you got desperate, you got tired, you got discouraged, you lost hope, etc. You might be in the darkest

THE UNNERVING DETOUR

detour of your life and still know that Jesus Christ is your God and Savior. He won't abandon you, no matter how undeserving you might be. I know that myself. Believe me.

So Jonah, knowing that he doesn't deserve anything good from God or his fellow travelers, told them to throw him overboard (verse 12). Eventually they did: "So they picked up Jonah, threw him into the sea, and the sea stopped its raging" (verse 15).

I don't know about you, but I have needed God's help to change the image of Him that had been imprinted on my brain. More than once, while taking a detour, I have mistakenly felt in the core of my soul that God was about to let me die as a punishment because I deserved it. I know . . . shocking, isn't it?

And yet this was not to be the end of God's wayward prophet. "The LORD appointed a great fish to swallow Jonah, and Jonah was in the stomach of the fish three days and three nights" (verse 17). Wait, what?

The unexpected way out

OK, so what do you do in the stomach of a really big fish for three days? As far as I know, there wasn't a single precedent for this experience; so how could Jonah know how to act in a situation like this? And I suppose there are not too many options to choose from in the belly of the fish. But one thing I do know: I would certainly pray. And that's what Jonah did. But this wasn't a "canned" prayer we sometimes resort to. Oh, no! This was a heartfelt psalm of thanksgiving for God's graceful deliverance.

Once Jonah was thrown from the ship, he was as good as dead. And he thought he was done. Who could have imagined Yahweh working out such a miraculous deliverance through a fish? "And the fish did not swallow him in order to eat him, *but to shelter him*."[2]

I love this phrase by Bible commentator Douglas Stuart: *not to eat him, but to shelter him.*[3] The fish did not come to get a meal but to offer a refuge. Yahweh (Jehovah), Jonah's God, was in total control and was not giving up on him, even though Jonah had taken an unnerving detour. He was still Jonah's God, and He was sticking to it!

I understand that we can't really explain this miracle, but that is the point of miracles—they are unexplainable to us. These are acts that only God understands and orchestrates. He is in total control of the sea and of the fish. He is God. And we are not.

Jonah prayed this psalm of thanksgiving to the Lord (Yahweh in the original), *his* God. Yahweh was still Jonah's only God, even though Jonah had been trying very hard to get away from Him. Now, Jonah recognized that God had delivered him from a sure death, and he started the psalm by acknowledging that.

"I called out of my distress to the LORD,
And He answered me.
I cried for help from the depth [literally *belly*] of Sheol;
You heard my voice" (Jonah 2:2).

Jonah continued to describe how he was surrounded by water in the depth of the sea; he was sure this was it! Take just a moment to read this amazing prayer (verses 2–9).

I love the last line, which we all need to repeat over and over again: "Salvation is from the LORD" (verse 9). That was Jonah's conclusion and should be ours too. When we are in the pit, in a hole that we have dug for ourselves, our only chance of survival comes from Him. Once Jonah acknowledged this, the fish vomited him on dry land (verse 10).

THE UNNERVING DETOUR

The bottom line of this prayer, which is the heart of the book of Jonah, is Jonah's acknowledgment that he is the recipient of God's grace, even though he doesn't deserve it. He needs deliverance, and he finds it only in God's graceful heart. So it turns out that the prophet, in fact, is in the same boat as the people of Nineveh. They both had messed up pretty badly and were in need of God's graceful deliverance. Therefore we assume that when God sends Jonah to Nineveh again, he should be super happy to see God extending His amazing grace to the Ninevites too, right? Well, not so much.

Salvation for *them*?

So Jonah found himself on the beach, covered in who knows what, and the word of the Lord came to him a second time and told him to go to Nineveh. This time Jonah went. He told the people that if they persisted in their ways, the city would be destroyed after forty days. "Then the people of Nineveh believed in God" (Jonah 3:5); they repented, and God relented and did not destroy them.

So Jonah was very happy that they received the same grace of God that he had received in the belly of the fish, right? Not really.

"But it greatly displeased Jonah and he became angry. He prayed to the LORD and said, 'Please LORD, was not this what I said while I was still in my own country? Therefore in order to forestall this I fled to Tarshish, for *I knew that You are a gracious and compassionate God, slow to anger and abundant in lovingkindness, and one who relents concerning calamity.* Therefore now, O LORD, please take my life from me, for death is better to me than life' " (Jonah 4:1–3; emphasis added).

Oh, come on! How stubborn could he be? First of all, Jonah acknowledged that he *knew* God was gracious and compassionate. Of course he knew! He was a recent recipient of God's grace and compassion. But he doesn't want the same grace for *them.*

Do you have a *them* in your life who you think doesn't deserve God's grace? Are you being sent by God to tell them that there is enough grace for them in the blood of Jesus that was shed for them at the cross?

Second, Jonah was so angry that he wanted to die. Again! He was so happy to have been delivered from death in chapter 2. Now he wanted to die because things were not going his way. Wow! Talk about rage. He was so angry that God had to help His obstinate prophet understand more about His grace and all-encompassing love through a little plant that He appointed (as He had appointed the fish). Read this amusing narrative in Jonah chapter 4.

In the last verse of the whole book, there is a wonderful statement about God's compassion that, in my view, summarizes the theme of this book: "Should I not have compassion on Nineveh, the great city in which there are more than 120,000 persons who do not know the difference between their right and left hand, as well as many animals?" (Jonah 4:11).

You see, God had compassion on Nineveh, not because they earned it but because of who He is. The Ninevites didn't deserve it. Neither did Jonah. No one does. Yet when we accept God's graceful offer to come to Him, at that very moment, we become the recipients of His salvation. We have such high worth in His eyes, no matter what we have done or how dark our detour, that He offers us salvation from the wages of our sin, which is death. The book of Jonah reminds us that God's grace is sufficient to cover all of us, even *them,* at our worst moments.

THE UNNERVING DETOUR

Will you accept it right here, right now? Jonah's experience in the belly of the fish would become a sign of what we call the *gospel*, and Jesus would later on refer to it specifically. Let me explain.

The sign of Jonah

Fast forward hundreds of years to when God became a human being in the person of Jesus in order to save us. One day some religious people were asking Him for a sign of who He was.

> Then some of the scribes and Pharisees said to Him, "Teacher, we want to see a sign from You." But He answered and said to them, "An evil and adulterous generation craves for a sign [or attesting miracle]; and yet no sign will be given to it but *the sign of Jonah the prophet*; for just as JONAH WAS THREE DAYS AND THREE NIGHTS IN THE BELLY OF THE SEA MONSTER, so will the Son of Man be three days and three nights in the heart of the earth. The men of Nineveh will stand up with this generation at the judgment, and will condemn it because they repented at the preaching of Jonah; and behold, something greater than Jonah is here" (Matthew 12:38–41; emphasis added).

Wow! OK, let's understand this a bit more.

The issue was not that the scribes and Pharisees were asking for a sign in order to believe. The issue was that in spite of all the miracles and signs, in the presence of such powerful evidence, they were *still* refusing to believe in Jesus. That's why Jesus was unwilling to perform a sign simply to show off His power. So He referred back to the place where Jonah had found God's grace in the belly of the fish and made a parallelism with the upcoming cross as the only legitimizing sign that could convince them of His grace. The Jewish way of counting days allows for three days, even though the first and the last of the three might be partial days. Regardless, the point was that Jesus would spend three days in the heart of the earth because He would die and be buried, then rise again. In this story we can find the true gospel, the real good news, that there is enough grace there to cover all of our most shameful detours.

Jesus reminded the religious leaders that the people of Nineveh repented when Jonah preached, and that something much greater than Jonah's proclamation was happening. Jesus, God in the flesh, was walking among them as the fulfillment of all the prophecies about the Messiah. And so it is for us. The cross was the ultimate legitimizing sign of who Jesus is and how He sees us. God's love for Jonah was greater than his detour. God's grace for the people of Nineveh was greater than their evil ways. God's compassion towards you and me is also greater than our darkest pits. So let's allow Him to deliver us from our shame and confusion. And let's utter a psalm of thanksgiving. Even in the middle of the storm, He sends a shelter for our bruised souls. He does this so that we can truly understand that salvation comes only from the Lord and is available to *all* of us! Oh, wow! Amazing grace, how sweet the sound that saved a wretch like me![4]

---

1. Parker J. Palmer, *On the Brink of Everything: Grace, Gravity, and Getting Old* (Oakland, CA: Berrett-Koehler, 2018).

2. Douglas Stuart, *Hosea-Jonah*, Word Biblical Commentary vol. 31 (Grand Rapids, MI: Zondervan, 1988), 474.

3. Douglas Stuart, *Hosea-Jonah*, 474.

4. John Newton, "Amazing Grace" (1779).

10. THE UNSETTLING WIND

Unsettling: Causing anxiety or uneasiness; disturbing.
—Oxford Dictionary

Has God ever asked you to do something that didn't make any sense? Have you ever had to go out on a limb with God? Let me share a bit about my experience in this area. I had been in ministry for several years and was a lead pastor at the time. I was having the time of my life when I started feeling that God was asking me to pause my ministry for a while to complete a PhD. I started sharing this with the leadership who appointed me to my ministerial position, and they all thought it wasn't a good idea at the time. The church was growing, the members were excited about studying the Scriptures together several times a week, everything seemed to be progressing as the gospel of Jesus Christ was being preached, and God's Spirit was dwelling powerfully with the membership.

But this feeling I had grew stronger and stronger, with the message that something big was coming in the future. The sense developed that I needed to take some time off to advance in my doctoral studies because when that big thing happened, I wouldn't have time to continue my studies. Mind you, I had no idea what that big thing was, and I couldn't understand why God would ask me to leave the ministry. This was especially true because I was the only female senior pastor in that geographical region at the time. Now I know that the big thing was the media ministry that I have been heading for the last fifteen years.*

It was obvious that God was sending a message to my heart, and I talked about it with the leaders of my local church. I distinctly remember a letter I received from one of them, explaining why this didn't make sense in light of all the positive experiences we were having at the church. I started to answer the letter, but I gave up. The reasons he gave me in his letter made a lot of sense, and my answers didn't. There was no plausible explanation for why God was asking me to do this at that moment. But soon after, the denominational leadership reluctantly gave me a leave to study.

And there I was, September 1, 2007, sitting on my living room sofa, writing my first jobless devotional prayer, saying to God: "I am going out on a limb with You. Today I have no job, no professional identity. I have never been without work during my whole adult life. Everything is unsure, yet I am certain You are asking me to do this, and I am willing to go out on a limb with You."

My husband and I took out a second mortgage on our house to survive financially during whatever time this "pause" would take. God was asking me to do something that didn't look possible and didn't make sense. Yet there I was, hoping that He would make it possible if, in fact, it was His voice that had commanded me to do it. The story in this chapter is deeply personal to me. Because every once in a while, God will command us to walk on water when we know for certain that we are incapable of doing it.

---

* For more information about the ministry, please visit Jesus101.tv or download the Jesus101 app.

THE UNSETTLING WIND

The uncommon storm

We live in a world that is filled with tempest-like situations, constantly reminding us about the effects of sin; therefore many of us have become pretty good at weathering storms. Yet, every now and then, we may face a storm so fierce, uncommon, or unsettling that it seems to laugh at our storm-weathering skills. We are no longer in control as the storm is way over our heads, and we fear we won't survive it. This was the kind of storm that the disciples met one day.

It had been an eventful day. Jesus had fed five thousand men, not including the women and children, by miraculously multiplying five loaves of bread and two fish (see Matthew 14:13–21). After it was over Jesus sent His disciples to the other side of the lake, while He, seeking solitude, stayed behind and went to a mountain to pray (verses 22, 23). Evening came, and that's when the disciples found themselves in trouble, a long distance from the shore.

Now, please remember that many of the disciples were fishermen. They had experienced storms before. In all likelihood they were quite skilled in storm-weathering. And yet, this time, their skills were no match for what they were encountering. Sound familiar?

"But the boat was already a long distance from the land, battered by the waves; *for the wind was contrary*" (Matthew 14:24; emphasis added). This phrase, "for the wind was contrary," caught my attention. The Greek word for *contrary* (*enantios*) is used only here in the gospel of Matthew. The wind is *adverse* to their plans for advancing. The wind is fighting *against* them. It is *opposite* to what it should be, the opposite to what they were expecting. And therefore the disciples are being tossed and harassed by the waves. This is an adversity of epic proportions, and they are helpless.

Can you relate? You thought that with strength and wit, with a positive attitude and intelligence, you would be able to meet the demands of the circumstances you are facing. And yet, because this is an uncommon storm, you feel helpless. But wait! An uncommon Help is about to enter the scene.

The uncommon help

The evening/night was divided into four watches: first watch was 6:00 P.M. to 9:00 P.M., second watch was 9:00 P.M. to midnight, third watch was midnight to 3:00 A.M., and fourth watch was 3:00 A.M. to 6:00 A.M. "And in the fourth watch of the night He came to them, walking on the sea" (verse 25). The fourth watch was 3:00 A.M. to 6:00 A.M., which meant the disciples were battling the stormy wind all night long!

Jesus had been praying most of the night as well. He came to the disciples by walking on the water, as if it was the most natural thing to do. God has always had dominion over the waves (see Job 9:8; Psalm 77:19; 107:28–30), and in this event Jesus revealed His supernatural side to the disciples. But as miraculous as Jesus' walking on the water was, we can't miss the point that He came to the disciples to help them in their distress. Yes, He came in an uncommon way, and He came because they needed Him. Let us not forget that Jesus always comes to aid us in our storms.

Instead of calming down, "when the disciples saw Him walking on the sea, they were terrified, and said, 'It is a ghost!' And they cried out in fear" (verse 26). The disciples thought Jesus was a ghost! The popular belief at the time was that evil

THE UNSETTLING WIND

spirits resided under the water, and this was probably what was on the disciples' minds. So much so that they couldn't stay quiet but cried out in fear. Having rowed against the adverse wind all night, the disciples were unable to recognize the uncommon Help that was coming their way.

Interesting, isn't it? When we are battling uncommon, unsettling, contrary winds, our minds are so wrapped up in fear that we often miss the presence of God with us. Sometimes the same happens to me. Have mercy on us, oh Lord!

"But immediately Jesus spoke to them, saying, 'Take courage, it is I; do not be afraid' " (verse 27). As the disciples were crying out, Jesus immediately identified Himself to relieve their fear. In Exodus 3:14 God revealed to Moses His covenantal name, "I AM." In the Greek translation of the Old Testament (LXX), the phrase was *ego eimi*. Guess what? These were the exact words Jesus used in Matthew 14:27—*ego eimi*, "It is I," "I am"—pointing to a deeper meaning about His identity.

I believe that in all the uncommon storms we face, God reveals Himself to us in a new, real, and personal way. I have learned more about God (and myself) in the storms and deserts of life than at any other point in my spiritual and emotional journey. In this case, as in many other instances in the Bible, the revelation of Jesus' identity was accompanied by the exhortation, "Do not fear." Why not? Why shouldn't we fear if we are in the midst of a storm we can't control? I am so glad you asked the question! It's because the only antidote to fear is God's presence with us.

These three parts in Jesus' statement are practical ways of stilling our anxious hearts: (1) *Take courage*. Don't despair, don't give up, be strengthened. Why? Because (2) *it is I*. It's

Me, the great I AM. I am with you; I am here, and you are not alone. I AM the God of the covenant who is here to help, and I will not let you go. Therefore (3) *do not be afraid.* Don't get anxious; don't let your heart be troubled. You have an antidote for your fear. The eternal loving God is with you, and He will see you through this storm.

Who knows, you might even have the most amazing experience of your life right here, right now, in the middle of the storm.

The uncommon experience
Peter, being quite unpredictable by nature, the type of person who's always ready to jump into the unknown, decided to find out if the one talking over the sound of the wind was really Jesus. "Peter said to Him, 'Lord, if it is You, *command me to come to You on the water*' " (verse 28; emphasis added).

Wait, what? Peter wanted to walk on water? What kind of a test was that? Well, one of Jesus' amazing characteristics is that He often shares His power and supernatural abilities with His followers, enabling them to do what they absolutely can't do on their own.

The only thing more surprising than Peter's request was Jesus' answer. "He said, 'Come!' And Peter got out of the boat, and walked on the water and came toward Jesus" (verse 29).

Wait, wait, wait! He did what? He walked on water? Yep, he most certainly did. In the midst of our uncommon storms, it's always good to remember that what is impossible for us is possible for God. And Peter walked on water simply because Jesus commanded him to do so. But we are feeble and failing human beings, and just when Peter thought he had a handle on it, he turned his attention to the wind.

THE UNSETTLING WIND

"But seeing the wind, he became frightened, and beginning to sink, he cried out, 'Lord, save me!' " (verse 30).

Can you relate? I certainly can! Remember that this was an uncommon, unsettling wind. It has happened to me so many times! Just when I think I finally have a handle on things, I have managed to develop my storm-weathering skills, I notice the wind.

Has it happened to you? Just when you think you are emotionally and spiritually strong, just when you become sure you have reached enough sobriety to never fall in the same hole again, that's exactly when it happens. You have a relapse; you have an outburst of rage; you have an affair; you visit an X-rated website; you gossip; you yell at your children and kick your dog. When you just started to take in the exhilarating sensation of walking on water, feeling so close to Jesus as never before, finally on the right path—*bam!* You see the wind, fear grasps your heart, and, once again, you start sinking in the dark waters of our sin-broken world. But don't despair! I have good news for you.

"Immediately Jesus stretched out His hand and took hold of him" (verse 31). Yes, you read it right! *Immediately!* Before any counsel or teaching or even a question, Jesus stretched out His hand and saved Peter.

I can't tell you how much this means to me. When I find myself in a dark pit, a raging storm, or a dry and lonely desert, I always know and believe that if, in my desperation, I turn to Christ, He will never cast me out but *immediately* will take a hold of me and remind me of His saving grace. Always. For the rest of my life.

I want to share with you a commentary on this verse that I found insightful and helpful:

"But Peter never finally failed, for always in the moment of his failure he clutched at Christ. The wonderful thing about him is that every time he fell, he rose again; and that it must have been true that even his failures brought him closer and closer to Jesus Christ. As has been well said, a saint is not a man who never fails; a saint is a man who gets up and goes on again every time he falls. Peter's failures only made him love Jesus Christ the more."[1]

Amen and amen! God knows that my failures, which have been many, have brought me greater revelations of God's grace for me. What happened to Peter and to me also will happen to you, for God truly reveals Himself as a compassionate and graceful God in the midst of our crisis.

The uncommon revelation

In His own compassionate and tender way, Jesus then brought up the fact that Peter's fear and doubts had something to do with his lack of faith (verse 31).

That is true of all of us as well. Jesus never abandons us when drowning, even if it is due to our little faith. This is one of the most encouraging truths of this story, one that I never want to forget.

"When they got into the boat, the wind stopped. And those who were in the boat *worshiped Him*, saying, '*You are certainly God's Son!*' " (verses 32, 33; emphasis added).

Wow! Can you imagine the scene? The disciples had a worship service in the middle of the lake, at the very place of the unsettling crisis moments before. In the midst of their storm, they had received a new revelation of who Jesus was. And the only natural response was to worship Him and praise Him as God's

THE UNSETTLING WIND

Son. God in the flesh was with them in the boat. Wow!

Everything about that night in the lake was uncommon. Yet, in the midst of it all, the disciples understood more about Jesus' identity and His ability to save to the uttermost, even those who fail when they see the wind.

Take heart my friend. No matter how frightened you feel, Jesus is standing next to you, ready to take hold of you and save you as soon as you let Him.

That evening the disciples witnessed the great miracle of Jesus walking on the water, which proved His divinity to them and motivated them to worship Him right then and there. Yet an even greater miracle happened at the cross. We had been eternally separated from God by the deep and dark sea of sin, never to dwell with Him again. Yet Jesus came to us, to our aid, in the most desperate of the human condition, and reached out to us, extending His graceful hand to save us. He lived a perfect life in our place, offered that perfect life on the cross for our sins, rose from the dead, and is soon coming to take us to live with Him forever. The cross was the greatest revelation of His love and grace toward us.

If you haven't done it yet, will you accept Jesus as your Savior right here and right now, in the middle of your crisis? Give your life to Him, and let Him fill your heart with His peace that is greater than our understanding of the situation we are in. He will reveal Himself to you in uncommon ways, and who knows, He might even command you to walk on water.

---

1. William Barclay, *The Gospel of Matthew: Chapters 11 to 28*, vol. 2, rev. ed., The Daily Study Bible (Edinburgh: Saint Andrew Press, 1975), 107.

11. THE UNAVOIDABLE SHIPWRECK

*Unavoidable: Inescapable, inevitable,
sure to happen, unpreventable.*
—Oxford Dictionary

When I was in my late twenties, I decided to open a computer company. This was no ordinary business project. I had bought the rights to computer software designed specifically for the automotive industry. I had worked for the company that originally designed it, teaching new buyers how to use this integrated system that contained literally hundreds of programs for stores that offered mechanic services while also selling auto parts to the public. It was quite innovative at the time, and after working a few years with it, I thought it was a good time to purchase the rights to the software and have my own clients. But then the storm came.

Even though I had quite a bit of experience operating the integrated multiuser software (before networks were a thing) and had a really good programmer working for me, it turned out that it was hard to compete with bigger companies that had similar integrated software but larger infrastructures. I thought I was ready, but it would have been wise to get more advice from people who had been in this business a bit longer. I was young and thought I could do anything. I tried really hard, even going out to do demos and sales, which was not the part I enjoyed the most in business. But no matter how hard I tried, it was becoming evident that things were not going as planned.

THE UNAVOIDABLE SHIPWRECK

Aside from the difficulty with the business, one day, as I was getting up from the office floor where I had been sitting, I crushed the meniscus of my right knee and had to have surgery that took me out of action for a few weeks. As months went by I began to worry that the company wasn't going to make it. And one day my heart started racing so fast that I ended up in the emergency room. That's when I decided that I had to put an end to it.

But many questions bombarded my mind. *What about the clients who were depending on the company for their software support? What should I do next? And where would I get the money to pay off investors? What would happen to the employees?* As far as I could tell, this was going to be a total shipwreck, and I was going to lose everything. And, really, what can sustain us in the middle of a storm where all of our best efforts are failing?

When real storms hit us, we literally don't see a way out. We can even lose our hope of deliverance from the crisis, especially when we have been in it for a while. That's why the story that we will analyze in this chapter is a great reminder of what to do when we are in a crisis, when we can't see the light at the end of the tunnel. Sometimes it feels like it is the end, but God is the Master of creating a way out when we don't see a path forward. And this is what happened to Paul, Luke, and the crew that was with them on the ship to Rome. It's quite a story! So let's get started.

When the plan doesn't work

Paul and Luke were on a ship bound for Italy (Acts 27:6). They were sailing slowly due to the wind and came to a place called Fair Havens on the island of Crete (verses 7, 8). The time was going by, and the fast (Day of Atonement) was already over, meaning it was around September or October. It was a dangerous time to travel, and Paul had some advice for those in charge: "Men, I perceive that the voyage will certainly be with damage and great loss, not only of the cargo and the ship, *but also of our lives*" (verse 10; emphasis added). But Paul's words didn't carry much weight with the centurion since the ship's captain thought otherwise. "Because the harbor [Fair Havens] was not suitable for wintering, the majority reached a decision to put out to sea from there, if somehow they could reach Phoenix, a harbor of Crete, facing southwest and northwest, and spend the winter there" (verse 12). The crew decided to try to reach Phoenix, a harbor on the same island of Crete that was better equipped to sustain them during the winter months.

Now, I want you to find a little map of this event. Fair Havens and Phoenix were very close to each other on the island of Crete, and their plan seemed somewhat appropriate. Like the TV comedy *Gilligan's Island*, which I liked as a kid, this journey was supposed to take only a few hours. Furthermore they were sailing along Crete, "close inshore" (verse 13) for protection. So what could go wrong, right? Well, everything that could go wrong went wrong.

The storms and winds that come to our lives and wreck our plans are always unexpected and bewildering, leaving us with our plans shattered and in total darkness without the faintest light at the end of the tunnel.

"But before very long there rushed down from the land a violent wind, called Euraquilo; and when the ship was caught in it and could not face the wind, we gave way to it and let ourselves be driven along" (verses 14, 15).

THE UNAVOIDABLE SHIPWRECK 107

Wait, what? You mean you can't control the ship because of the strength of the wind? Oh, yeah! You know exactly what I am talking about. That's exactly what a crisis is. And this was no ordinary wind.

Help! We are not going to make it!

Several years ago my parents, my husband, and I went on a tour called "In the Footsteps of Paul." It was an amazing trip that included such places as Athens, Corinth, Thessaloniki, Berea, and others. We also were scheduled to spend three days on a medium-sized ship in the Mediterranean Sea. And you are going to laugh about my next sentence: I scheduled our trip at a time of the year when I was certain we would miss the *Euraquilo* mentioned in Acts 27:14. Isn't that something? This northeastern wind has hurricane force, and, as far as I understand, it is still around nowadays. In this story it truly caused some havoc. So much so that the crew's best efforts to survive were rendered meaningless.

And speaking of efforts, the next few verses talk in detail about all the attempts they made to try to face this unstoppable storm. This is what I call "a developmental progression of hopelessness and despair."

Can you relate? You escalate your commitment, but the harder you try, the more you lose. And, little by little, hopelessness sets in.

The sailors, like us, were bargaining with the storm, trying everything they could think of. First, they tried to get the ship's lifeboat under control (verse 16). This was usually a little boat that enables the crew to get to shore when the big ship is anchored. So they tried to secure it. After they did that, they used "supporting cables in undergirding the ship" (verse 17), trying to prevent it from breaking up into pieces. They let down the sea anchor, but nothing was working. This was quite a struggle for survival, wasn't it? But soon they realized it wasn't working.

"The next day as we were violently storm-tossed, they began to jettison the cargo; and on the third day they threw the ship's tackle overboard with their own hands. Since neither sun nor stars appeared for many days, and no small storm was assailing us, from then on *all hope of our being saved was gradually abandoned*" (verses 18–20; emphasis added).

Sound familiar? *All hope gradually abandoned!* Wow! I've heard it said, and I agree, that the hardest trials are usually the longer trials when you don't see the end in sight. Little by little, all hope is gradually abandoned. But wait! A message was about to be delivered that would bring much-needed hope.

The message

"When they had gone a long time without food, then Paul stood up in their midst" (verse 21). You can imagine why they had gone quite a while without food, because who can hold anything down after days of being tossed by the waves? But, most importantly, Paul had a message for the sailors. The first thing he says is a sort of "I told you so," which I think reveals a little about Paul's personality. They should have listened to him when he admonished them not to set sail from Crete (see verse 21). And then comes the news that he wants to share with them:

"Yet now I urge you to keep up your courage, for there will be no loss of life among you, but only of the ship. For this very night an angel of the God to whom I belong and whom

THE UNAVOIDABLE SHIPWRECK

I serve stood before me, saying, 'Do not be afraid, Paul; you must stand before Caesar; and behold, God has granted you all those who are sailing with you.' Therefore, keep up your courage, men, for I believe God that it will turn out exactly as I have been told" (verses 22–25).

Wow! How is that for a super encouraging message? Woo-hoo!

Even though back in verse 10 Paul thought there would be a loss of life, he now had new information, and there wasn't going to be any loss of life. Sometimes the presence of one person who belongs to God makes a difference for a whole company of people, and that was the case this time. God granted Paul the life of all who were with him on the ship. Amazing!

I feel validated by the first few words of the angel: "Do not be afraid, Paul" (verse 24). Somehow Paul didn't strike me as a person who got scared easily, yet long storms get to the best of us. So the first thing the angel does is address Paul's fear. God still had an important purpose to achieve: Paul was to appear before Caesar. The message ended with Paul inspiring his fellow travelers to "keep up [their] courage" (verse 25) because he truly believed that the message he had received was true and everything would happen as he had been told.

In other words, in spite of the storm, choose faith over fear because we know how the story ends! By the way, God has already revealed to us the final chapters of our story as well.

After delivering the message, Paul did something that might surprise you.

Church on the water

"But when the fourteenth night came . . ." (verse 27).

Wait, what? Do you mean that they had been in the storm for fourteen days without hope nor sunshine? Yep! Fourteen days on the sea, being tossed by the waves; fourteen weeks waiting for an answer to your confusion; fourteen months with cancer, chemo, and radiation; fourteen years feeding your handicapped child through a tube . . . Oh, yes! A long time without an end in sight.

All of a sudden the men took soundings, and they realized they were approaching land. They cast four anchors to avoid crushing the ship on the rocks. But some sailors got a little too desperate and, since they seemed to be close to the shore, tried to lower the ship's lifeboat to get away. But Paul spoke up.

"Paul said to the centurion and to the soldiers, 'Unless these men remain in the ship, you yourselves cannot be saved.' Then the soldiers cut away the ropes of the ship's boat and let it fall away" (verses 31, 32).

This was going to be done God's way. Human effort had already failed in their previous attempts to save themselves, and now God was taking over. It wasn't going to be a little bit of God and a little bit of men. It was going to be all or nothing. All God. No human ingenuity nor strength. Just like salvation. It is done only God's way. It's not that we need a little help, some grace, to be saved. It is all and only grace. Period.

This reminds me of an enlightening paragraph in one of Max Lucado's books, discussing the meeting of the first-century church in Acts 15 and their struggle to understand this "grace alone" concept:

THE UNAVOIDABLE SHIPWRECK

It wasn't that the people didn't believe in grace at all. They did. They believed in grace a lot. They just didn't believe in grace alone. They wanted to add to the work of Christ.

Grace-a-lots believe in grace, a lot. Jesus almost finished the work of salvation, they argue. In the rowboat named *Heaven Bound*, Jesus paddles most of the time. But every so often he needs our help. So we give it.[1]

Back to our story. Paul said that the sailors needed to trust what God said regarding how they were going to be saved (and so do we). Then he encouraged them to eat, and Luke told this part of the story in a very interesting way:

"Paul was encouraging them all to take some food, saying, 'Today is the fourteenth day that you have been constantly watching and going without eating, having taken nothing. Therefore I encourage you to take some food, for this is for your preservation, *for not a hair from the head of any of you will perish*.' Having said this, *he took bread and gave thanks to God in the presence of all, and he broke it and began to eat*. All of them were encouraged and they themselves also took food" (verses 33–36; emphasis added).

OK, let me unpack this a bit. First of all, Paul reminded the sailors of the end result: "not a hair from the head of any of you will perish" (verse 34). Even though God had decided not to calm the storm this time, He sent the message that this particular storm was not going to destroy their lives. Wow! It makes such a difference to go through something knowing how it will end.

The second part I want to point out is that Luke used words associated with Jesus' Last Supper for the meal Paul and the sailors took. These were the same words used when Jesus took bread, gave thanks, broke it, and gave it to the disciples (see Luke 22:14–20). Some churches call this event the *Eucharist* (from the Greek verb *eucharisteo*: to "give thanks"), remembering when Jesus took bread and wine to represent His body and blood that would be broken and shed for us at the cross. We still celebrate the Lord's Supper to this day, to remember what He did for us, and to announce His death until His second coming (see 1 Corinthians 11:23–26). In other words, in this passage, Luke was giving us the not-so-subtle message that when we are in the midst of our crisis, we are to trust what Jesus has already done for us and the promises that come with that.

You'll get through it

Newsflash: the outcome is not in our hands. We can't control it. We can't stop the shipwreck. We might feel powerless, but the good news is that God is powerful and He cares for us. This is demonstrated at the cross, where He laid down His perfect life to pay for our transgressions. He then rose from the dead, and we have the guarantee of His Presence every day until the very end of the world. If, at any point, He chooses not to calm a particular storm, then He promises to get us through it.

In case you were wondering, I did close the computer company that I mentioned in the introduction. It took a while to get everything in order, but I made it by God's grace.

As the narrative of the unavoidable shipwreck continues, we learn that there were 276 persons on that ship (see Acts 27:37). After so many days of super stormy weather, the sailors ran the vessel aground, and, holding on to planks and other

THE UNAVOIDABLE SHIPWRECK 113

things from the ship, they made their way to shore. And I love how the narrative ends: "And so it happened that they all were brought safely to land" (verse 44).

"And so it happened" because God was in it; otherwise they wouldn't have made it. I can't wait for all believers to be standing by the sea of glass in the heavenly Promised Land and hear this sentence: "And so it happened that they all were brought safely to the promised land."

We already know the end of the story: *Jesus wins!* And we are with Him. So don't despair (I am preaching to myself right now). Focus on the broken body of Jesus on the cross and His shed blood on your behalf. Let Him encourage you, even if you are in the middle of your worst and darkest storm. He will reveal Himself to you in relevant, personal, and real ways just when you are starting to abandon all hope of survival—just like He did for Paul. Because God also wants to make a Bible story out of your life.

---

1. Max Lucado, *Grace: More Than We Deserve, Greater Than We Imagine* (Nashville, TN: Thomas Nelson, 2012), 45.

12. THE UNCHARTED DESERT

Uncharted: Not mapped or surveyed. Unexplored.
—Oxford Dictionary

Since becoming an adult, I often suffered from unusual stomach problems. Sometimes my stomach would react violently to a particular food or unknown virus, and the reaction potentially would disable me for several days. Thankfully this has gotten better with age. But I remember one time when an extreme case of this condition rendered me helpless.

I was on a ministerial retreat at a beautiful resort and was really enjoying my time with fellow ministers and with God. All of a sudden my stomach started feeling funny, and then the ordeal started. Between the vomiting and diarrhea, I lost about ten pounds within a few hours and could barely move, let alone hold down any food or drink.

Paramedics were called. They saw my severe condition but said they could not administer an IV due to the forest area we were in (which I still don't understand). They said I should try to drink liquids and rest to gain some strength to be transported. One of the pastors on the retreat was very compassionate and tried to give me something to eat and drink, but I couldn't hold anything down.

The issue was that the retreat was ending, everyone was leaving, and I was not strong enough to make the trip back. In addition, we didn't know how long it was going to take for me to get back on my feet. But even if it took two or three days, I

THE UNCHARTED DESERT

wouldn't have a ride back home because I had carpooled with the same people who were now leaving. So I called my parents.

I knew that my parents were always ready and willing to step in, no matter what. And even though they lived many hours away from where I was, within a few minutes of getting my call, they were on the road headed in my direction. Wow! I will be forever thankful to heaven for the privilege of having godly parents.

After driving for six or seven hours, my parents arrived at the resort. They had brought everything so they could stay with me for as long as needed and nurse me back to health. And they did. After a couple of days, they made a "bed" in their van, and I lay down to make the trip home.

By telling this story I want to point out that my parents were *always* available for me unconditionally. Many times they did for me what I couldn't do for myself. They rescued me from accidents or almost-drowning events when I was a child, and from situations of illness or financial difficulties all the way into my adulthood. When I lost both of them to cancer, I also lost that unconditional, protective blanket that I had always counted on.

In this last story of *Storms and Deserts*, I want to talk about the One who has done for us what we could have never done for ourselves. The One who offers us His unconditional help at all times and in all circumstances, even if we are the ones who caused the storm we are in. And this is the only reason we can go through this world's darkest crises with assurance and not despair.

I want to share with you the meaning of this reality, because none of us has a perfect way of going through the storms and deserts of life. We make tons of mistakes in the process; at least I know I do. We are human beings, and humans inevitably make mistakes. Often we feel handicapped and helpless in our condition. That's why our "certainty" in times of difficulties cannot come from ourselves. It comes from Him who has overcome in our place. And He went through an uncharted wilderness just for us.

Who is He? Who am I?

Matthew recorded the baptism of Jesus at the very beginning of His public ministry (see Matthew 3:13–17). Then he added something astonishing: "After being baptized, Jesus came up immediately from the water; and behold, the heavens were opened, and he saw the Spirit of God descending as a dove and lighting on Him, and behold, a voice out of the heavens said, '*This is My beloved Son, in whom I am well-pleased*' " (verses 16, 17; emphasis added).

I find this statement fascinating! Before Jesus entered the uncharted desert of temptation, God reminded Him of His identity. He was God's beloved Son. He was a Son, He was beloved, and God claimed Him as His own. I believe that many of us would enter our storms and deserts with a completely different mindset if we were certain of our identity. I know I would. I believe this audible statement from God had a lot to do with Jesus' ability to face the temptations that the devil threw His way. I will explain that further in a few paragraphs.

So the question is, Am I certain of who I am in Christ? Are you? Do I always remember that I am God's beloved daughter because my identity is secure in what Jesus has done for me?

Recently someone shared an insight with me from a book

THE UNCHARTED DESERT

called *The Normal Christian Life*[1] that impacted her life. She commented: "I have three children. If one of them misbehaves, it does not mean that I only have two children that day. We don't say, 'Even though I had three children yesterday, because one of them is misbehaving today, I no longer count him as my child.' "

So true! We don't lose our identity as children of God because we are in a perplexing season, in the midst of confusion, depression, or discouragement. We continue to be God's beloved children. And as long as we remember that, we will never feel alone in the desert. As a matter of fact, we already know how our story ends.

Our story is His-story

One of the most important theological premises of the Gospel of Matthew was that Jesus relived Israel's history and was victorious where the Israelites had failed. Meaning that Israel's history of failure was being replaced by Jesus' perfect life, as is the case with us. Matthew made this point in several ways. For example, the introduction to the narrative of Jesus' desert experience closely resembled the narrative of the experience that Israel had in the wilderness back in Deuteronomy, where the Israelites failed miserably in trusting God.

So that you can see how deliberately Matthew chose words that would remind his audience of Israel's experience, I will include both introductions here. First, Matthew 4:1, 2: "Then Jesus was *led* up by the Spirit into the *wilderness* to be *tempted* by the devil. And after He had fasted *forty* days and *forty* nights, He then became *hungry*" (emphasis added).

Now, Deuteronomy 8:2, 3: "You shall remember all the way

which the LORD your God has *led* you in the *wilderness* these *forty* years, that He might humble you, *testing* you. . . . He humbled you and let you be *hungry*, and fed you with manna" (emphasis added).

Do you see how both introductions use similar words? But wait! There is so much more! In order to get the full impact of what Matthew is doing in this narrative, you need to have your Bible opened in two places: Matthew 4 and Deuteronomy 6–8.

Before we continue with the rest of the narrative, please pause with me for a moment to internalize what this theological premise means to us: When I accept Jesus Christ as my personal Savior, His perfect life and death are placed on my record as if they were my life and death. My story has already been written. It is history. My story is His story.

You can choose the worst week, month, year, or decade of your life and know that God sees it as perfect because of Jesus' record in your file. When Jesus is your Savior, the worst mistake you might have made—the affair, the abortion, the addiction, and so forth—is not counted against you. No wonder David, who made a lot of mistakes, talked about this incredible blessing! "How blessed is he whose transgression is forgiven, whose sin is covered! How blessed is the man to whom the LORD does not impute iniquity" (Psalm 32:1, 2; see also Romans 4:7, 8, where Paul uses these verses to explain being declared right with God by faith, not by our own works). This brings such blessed assurance to our hearts, doesn't it? He is the victorious One, and He did it in our place! Wow!

His retroactive victory

Jesus was entering an uncharted desert. It was uncharted not

THE UNCHARTED DESERT

because no one had walked this geographical area before but because there was no one who had been completely victorious over temptation and sin, ever. As mentioned previously, Matthew introduced this narrative with words similar to the introduction of Deuteronomy 8. He also carefully pointed out that all of Jesus' answers to the tempter were quotations from Deuteronomy 6–8, which narrated Israel's failure in the desert. This is captivating, and I want to make sure we don't miss a single word of it.

After fasting for forty days, Jesus became hungry, "and the tempter came and said to Him, 'If You are the Son of God, command that these stones become bread.' But He answered and said, 'It is written, "MAN SHALL NOT LIVE ON BREAD ALONE, BUT ON EVERY WORD THAT PROCEEDS OUT OF THE MOUTH OF GOD" ' " (Matthew 4:3, 4). Wow!

This quotation comes from Deuteronomy 8:3, following the introduction that we already looked at. Check it out: "He humbled you and let you be hungry, and fed you with manna which you did not know, nor did your fathers know, that He might make you understand that *man does not live by bread alone, but man lives by everything that proceeds out of the mouth of the* LORD" (emphasis added).

Did you see that? Fascinating! Jesus was quoting the Scriptures exactly from the experience of Israel in the desert, except that He was victorious where the Israelites had failed. Woo-hoo! This retroactive victory of Jesus on behalf of His people is also applied to us when we accept Him. Can you believe it?

It is enlightening to analyze how the first temptation started, questioning the very identity of Jesus: "*If* You are the Son of

God" (Matthew 4:3; emphasis added). The whole temptation was based on getting Jesus to *second-guess* who He was. The devil already knew who Jesus was. Yet the tempter wanted Him to *prove* that He was, in fact, the Son of God by turning stones into bread. Jesus was sure of His identity as the beloved Son of God and didn't need to prove anything to the devil or to Himself. He knew it, and He believed it. He was the Son, He was beloved, and He was God's. That was His story, and He was sticking to it!

We could call this the temptation of *achievement*. Somewhere along the path, many of us picked up the idea that we need to achieve something or show some good work in order to prove that we are children of God. But Jesus showed us that this temptation is met with a word from God and not with our showing off. God says I am His child, and therefore, I am His child. Period.

Satan, get out of here!

The second and third temptations were met with similar quotations from the same section of Scripture.

> Then the devil took Him into the holy city and had Him stand on the pinnacle of the temple, and said to Him, "*If You are the Son of God*, throw Yourself down; for it is written,
>
> 'He will command His angels concerning you';
> and
> 'On their hands they will bear You up,
> So that You will not strike Your foot against a stone'" (verses 5, 6; emphasis added).

THE UNCHARTED DESERT

OK, now the devil got smart. Still questioning, "If you are the Son of God," the adversary started quoting Scripture, in this case Psalm 91:11, 12.

Did you know that the devil can use Scripture against you to accuse you? He is the mega accuser, and he will use anything, even the Bible, to make you feel ashamed of yourself and to make you think you went too far.

But Jesus answered him with another Scripture, from the same section of Israel's failure as in the first temptation. "Jesus said to him, 'On the other hand, it is written, "YOU SHALL NOT PUT THE LORD YOUR GOD TO THE TEST" ' " (Matthew 4:7).

This quotation comes from Deuteronomy 6:16: "You shall not put the LORD your God to the test, as you tested Him at Massah."

I call this the temptation of religious *arrogance*. When you want to test God's Word on your own terms, whether privately or publicly, to see if it is true, it is called *presumption*. It is not true faith in times of need. Sometimes it takes the form of "showing off" in order to elicit applause or accolades. Other times it is the temptation to test if His words are true or not according to your own measurement.

The devil made a third and final attempt. "Again, the devil took Him to a very high mountain and showed Him all the kingdoms of the world and their glory; and he said to Him, 'All these things I will give You, if You fall down and worship me.' Then Jesus said to him, 'Go, Satan! For it is written, "YOU SHALL WORSHIP THE LORD YOUR GOD, AND SERVE HIM ONLY." ' Then the devil left Him" (Matthew 4:8–11).

In this final temptation, once again, Jesus answered from Israel's experience. "You shall fear only the LORD your God;

and you shall worship Him" (Deuteronomy 6:13). The Israelites had gotten confused about who (or what) to worship. Sometimes we do too.

I call this the temptation of *authority* or control. The devil thought he could "give" Jesus the kingdoms of this world. But Jesus was going to recover humankind through the Cross, not through some kind of authoritarian regime. Satan's way is always coercive, using force, threats, and false authority. I like the way Philip Yancey explains it:

> The Temptation in the desert reveals a profound difference between God's power and Satan's power. Satan has the power to coerce, to dazzle, to force obedience, to destroy. Humans have learned much from that power, and governments draw deeply from its reservoir. With a bullwhip or a billy club or an AK-47, human beings can force other human beings to do just about anything they want. Satan's power is external and coercive.
>
> God's power, in contrast, is internal and noncoercive. "You would not enslave man by a miracle, and craved faith given freely, not based on miracle," said the Inquisitor to Jesus in Dostoevsky's novel. Such power may seem at times like weakness. In its commitment to transform gently from the inside out and in its relentless dependence on human choice, God's power may resemble a kind of abdication. As every parent and every lover knows, love can be rendered powerless if the beloved chooses to spurn it.[2]

God never works by imposing violence, fear, or control. He motivates us intrinsically—with His love. Jesus gave up His

THE UNCHARTED DESERT

divine prerogative and humbled Himself to die on a cross for us. Humility, not authoritarianism, is God's way. And even in this area, Jesus was victorious where we have failed miserably.

It was time for Satan to leave. And Jesus told him so! "Go, Satan! We are done here. I know who I am. I AM the Son of God!"

The greatest assurance

It is imperative to understand that the temptations presented to Jesus were related to who and whose He was, and if He would trust God's way or not. By now you probably realized that all the titles I gave the three temptations start with an A: *achievement, arrogance, authority*. I believe that the main reason Jesus didn't fall into these temptations was another word that also starts with an A: *assurance*.

Jesus was sure of who and whose He was. He didn't need to prove His identity to the devil, to others, or to Himself. He knew, believed, and acted upon the fact that He was, and is, the Son of God. He heard God announce it from heaven (see Matthew 3:17), and He believed it in His heart and mind. He wasn't trying to fill that God-shaped hole in His heart with anything other than God.

It is extremely interesting to me that on the cross Jesus experienced the same temptation: to doubt if He was the Son of God. "*If You are the Son of God*, come down from the cross" (Matthew 27:40; emphasis added). Wow! To the very last minute of His earthly life, Jesus was mocked, spit upon, and ridiculed. Yet the greatest temptation was to doubt His identity and to come down from the cross to prove He was the Son of God.

Jesus loved us above Himself. He refused to go through eternity without you and me and therefore refused to come down from the cross—not because He couldn't but because He didn't want to. He lived a perfect life in our place and laid down that perfect life to pay the penalty for our sins. He humbled Himself for you and for me.

"Have this attitude in yourselves which was also in Christ Jesus, who, although He existed in the form of God, did not regard equality with God a thing to be grasped, but emptied Himself, taking the form of a bond-servant, and being made in the likeness of men. Being found in appearance as a man, He humbled Himself by becoming obedient to the point of death, even death on a cross" (Philippians 2:5–8).

Jesus rose from the dead on the third day and is soon to return for us, to take us to a place with no sin, death, disease, or crisis of any type. He is the One who was victorious in everything we failed in. Like my parents instilled in me their unconditional love for me as their child, Jesus wants us to live with the greatest assurance: that we are children of God (see 1 John 3:1; John 1:12, 13). Nothing can take away His victory on our behalf. If you have never accepted Jesus as your personal Savior, do so today.*

Jesus went through this uncharted desert for us. There is no other human being that was without sin, not before and not after. All have sinned! The apostle Paul clearly stated the bad news that we are sinners and the good news that, in spite of our nature, we are saved through Jesus: "For all have sinned and fall

---

* If you would like to receive a series of free Bible studies from Jesus 101, please contact us through our website www.Jesus101.tv, and we will be delighted to send it to you.

THE UNCHARTED DESERT

short of the glory of God, being justified [declared right with God] as a gift by His grace through the redemption which is in Christ Jesus" (Romans 3:23, 24).

I want to invite you to live with the greatest assurance. When you accept Jesus, you become a child of God. From then on that is your identity, regardless of whether you are on the top of the mountain or in the deepest valley. Whether you find yourself taking the darkest detour of despair or are experiencing the most successful season of your life. Nothing, no crisis whatsoever, can take away the love of Christ for you. And all because He loved us and won the battle of salvation on our behalf.

Repeat with me this statement from Paul, adding in the blank space whatever crisis you find yourself in.

"I'm absolutely convinced that nothing—nothing living or dead, angelic or demonic, today or tomorrow, high or low, thinkable or unthinkable [no crisis, no storm, no desert, no _____]—absolutely *nothing* can get between us and God's love because of the way that Jesus our Master has embraced us" (Romans 8:38, 39, *The Message*).

Woo-hoo!

---

1. Watchman Nee, *The Normal Christian Life* (Peabody, MA: Hendrickson Publishers, 1961).

2. Phillip Yancey, *The Jesus I Never Knew* (Grand Rapids, MI: Zondervan, 1995), 76.

CONCLUSION

Yes, we all struggle with major questions and pain. This is why our souls yearn for a better world without suffering, promised for those who accept Jesus as their Savior (see Revelation 21:4). But until then, while we still face the storms and conflicts of life here and now, God comes to us with compassion and grace. He reveals Himself to us in true and real ways, ministering to our souls and healing our wounds with a love and care that surpass our understanding, little by little changing our image of who He is.

I resonate with Phillip Yancey's statement: "I tend to write as a means of confronting my own doubts. . . . I return again and again to the same questions, as if fingering an old wound that never quite heals. Does God care about the misery down here? Do we really matter to God?"[1] I have never struggled with these types of questions more than during the last few years. Several things have happened in my life, including Patrick's prolonged neurological illness and the abandonment that I have felt, as the husband that I knew disappeared little by little, day after day, year after year. In the midst of all my preaching, teaching, broadcasting, taping and writing, God comforted me in a still small voice and "baked cakes" for me, as He did for Elijah in the midst of his exhaustion. My God, who never leaves us nor abandons us, continues to be merciful to me, even while my mind, at times, seems to be shaped in a giant question mark.

God shows up, and will continue to show up, not only as the

CONCLUSION

Savior who purchased my eternal salvation at the cross, but also as the very-present help in trouble (see Psalm 46:1). He yearns to reveal Himself to us in our storms and deserts, so that we may understand more and more about His grace and love for us. He sees us, hears us, and comes to our aid. Furthermore, no storm, no desert, no confusion, no detour, no pit, no question or discouragement will ever separate us from His love.

As I highlighted in the last chapter, we have an unshakable assurance: "I'm absolutely convinced that nothing—nothing living or dead, angelic or demonic, today or tomorrow, high or low, thinkable or unthinkable—absolutely *nothing* can get between us and God's love because of the way that Jesus our Master has embraced us" (Romans 8:38, 39, *The Message*).

Be encouraged, my fellow pilgrim, the eternal God walks with you, embracing you with His grace in the midst of your worst crises. Believe me, I have witnessed it! That's my story, and I am sticking to it.[2]

---

1. Phillip Yancey, *The Jesus I Never Knew* (Grand Rapids, MI: Zondervan, 1995), 17.

2. Don't forget to check out the videos that accompany each one of the chapters in this book (upcoming release in 2026).

For additional FREE resources, videos on demand, daily devotionals, biblical studies, audiobooks, and much more, please visit our website:

www.Jesus101.tv

If you have been blessed by this booklet and would like to receive free Bible Studies, please contact us through our website or write to us at

Jesus 101 Biblical Institute
PO Box 10008
San Bernardino, CA 92423

WATCH the JESUS 101 channel on YOUTUBE!

DOWNLOAD the JESUS 101 app TODAY!